William F. Buckley, Jr.

Twayne's United States Authors Series

Warren French, Editor
Indiana University, Indianapolis

TUSAS 452

WILLIAM F. BUCKLEY, JR.
(1925–   )
Photograph courtesy of
William F. Buckley, Jr.

William F. Buckley, Jr.

By Mark Royden Winchell

University of Southern Mississippi

Twayne Publishers • *Boston*

810.81
B 924 w

William F. Buckley, Jr.

Mark Royden Winchell

Copyright © 1984 by G. K. Hall & Company
All Rights Reserved
Published by Twayne Publishers
A Division of G. K. Hall & Company
70 Lincoln Street
Boston, Massachusetts 02111

Book Production by Marne B. Sultz

Book Design by Barbara Anderson

Printed on permanent/durable acid-free
paper and bound in the United States of
America.

Library of Congress Cataloging in Publication Data

Winchell, Mark Royden, 1948–
   William F. Buckley, Jr.

   (Twayne's United States authors series ; TUSAS 452)
   Bibliography: p. 152
   Includes index.
   1. Buckley, William F. (William Frank), 1925–
—Criticism and interpretation. I. Title. II. Series.
PS3552.U344Z95   1984   818'.5409   83-18224
ISBN 0-8057-7392-4
ISBN 0-8057-7431-9 (pbk)

For Tim, Missy, and Robin Marie Winchell

Contents

About the Author

Mark Royden Winchell received his B.A. and M.A. degrees in English from West Virginia University and his Ph.D. in English from Vanderbilt University. His work has appeared in the *American Spectator*, the *Sewanee Review*, the *Mississippi Quarterly*, the *Canadian Review of American Studies*, the *Ohio Journal*, the *South Central Bulletin*, the *University Bookman*, *Christianity and Literature*, the *Southern Humanities Review*, *Western American Literature*, the *Journal of Country Music*, the *New Oxford Review*, and other journals. In addition, he has contributed to several books, including *A History of Southern Literature*, *Los Angeles in Fiction*, *Contemporary Literary Criticism*, *Shakespeare in the South*, and the third edition of William Rose Benet's *Reader's Encyclopedia*. His major publications are a Twayne Series study of Joan Didion and a monograph on Horace McCoy in the Boise State University Western Writers Series. He currently teaches English and American Studies at the University of Southern Mississippi and is editing a special issue of the *Southern Quarterly* entitled *Country Music: Tradition and the Individual Talent*.

Preface

During the time that I was working on the following study, the two questions which I encountered most frequently were (1) Why write a book on Bill Buckley? and (2) Why hasn't someone done so already?

The answer to the first of these questions is relatively easy: William F. Buckley, Jr. is one of our most prolific and influential contemporary writers. As such, he has generated considerable public interest. Surprisingly, however, the vast preponderance of commentary published on him consists of personality profiles and contemporaneous book reviews. Thus far, the only *books* which have given him more than passing mention are Charles Lam Markmann's *The Buckleys: A Family Examined* and Mitchell S. Ross's *The Literary Politicians*. The first of these is a superficial hatchet job on the entire family, while the second treats Buckley as only one of six major figures, and several minor ones, who "practice politics by writing books." Clearly, there is a need for a full-length general introduction to Buckley's literary career. This book was written to satisfy that need.

The first of the following chapters offers a brief sketch of Buckley's life, and the second a discussion of his basic philosophy. At the other end of the study, we have an analysis of his four novels (chapter 13) and a tentative conclusion (chapter 14). In between are ten chapters which focus on various subjects and personalities which have engaged Buckley's attention. For the most part, then, I have taken a thematic approach to the corpus of Buckley's writings rather than pursue a volume-by-volume critique. My intention has been to examine continuity and development within the Buckley canon and to convey some sense of the breadth and flavor of the material being discussed.

In the last analysis, this book will have accomplished its purpose if those who read it understand why it was written and continue to be surprised that it had not been done a long time ago.

Mark Royden Winchell

University of Southern Mississippi

Acknowledgments

I wish to acknowledge several persons without whose valued assistance this book would not have appeared in its present form.

Mr. William F. Buckley, Jr. verified factual assertions and has also permitted me to use the quotations from his work which appear throughout this book. All of his material is copyrighted under his own name. Professor Wesley D. Anderson and Mr. William J. Studer of the Ohio State University helped provide access to needed resources. Lenora Ladner, Karen Greer, and Bonnie Campbell rendered important technical service. I am also grateful to Mr. James Calland and Ms. Cheryl Saunders for reading and commenting on the manuscript, to my parents for supplying encouragement and moral support, and to the University of Southern Mississippi for granting me released time to work on this project. Finally, Warren French has once again proved to be a discerning critic and a faithful friend.

Chronology

1925   William Frank Buckley, Jr. born in New York City, November 24; son of William Frank Buckley, Sr. and Aloise Steiner Buckley.

1943   Enters the University of Mexico.

1944–1946   Serves as second lieutenant in the United States Army.

1946   Enters Yale University.

1949–1950   Chairman of the *Yale Daily News*.

1950   Graduates from Yale. Marries Patricia Taylor.

1951   *God and Man at Yale.*

1951–1952   Works for the CIA in Mexico.

1952   Associate editor of the *American Mercury.*

1953   Son Christopher is born.

1954   *McCarthy and His Enemies* (with L. Brent Bozell).

1955   *National Review* founded.

1959   *Up From Liberalism.*

1960   Young Americans for Freedom founded.

1961   New York State Conservative Party founded.

1962   *The Committee and its Critics.* Begins weekly newspaper column *On the Right.*

1963   *Rumbles Left and Right.*

1964   Newspaper column expanded to three times a week. Barry Goldwater loses presidential election to Lyndon Johnson.

1965   Runs on the Conservative Party ticket for mayor of New York City; wins 13.4 percent of the vote in three-way race with John Lindsay and Abraham Beame.

1966   *The Unmaking of a Mayor.* Begins weekly television series *Firing Line.*

1968   *The Jeweler's Eye.* Appears with Gore Vidal on ABC-TV during Republican and Democratic National Conventions.

1969   Appointed by President Nixon to the U.S. Advisory Commission on Information. *Odyssey of a Friend.*

1970   *The Governor Listeth; Did You Ever See a Dream Walking?.* Brother James elected to the United States Senate from New York.

1971   *Cruising Speed.*

1972   *Inveighing We Will Go.* Resigns from Advisory Commission on Information as protest against leftist drift of Nixon administration.

1973   *Four Reforms.* Appointed by President Nixon to the U.S. Delegation to the United Nations.

1974   *United Nations Journal.*

1975   *Execution Eve.*

1976   *Saving the Queen.* James Buckley loses Senate seat to Daniel Patrick Moynihan. *Airborne.*

1978   *Stained Glass. A Hymnal.*

1980   *Who's On First.* Ronald Reagan elected president.

1982   *Marco Polo, If You Can. Atlantic High.*

1983   *Overdrive*

Chapter One
Biographia Literaria

His personal friend and ideological foe Norman Mailer says of William F. Buckley: "No other actor on earth can project simultaneous hints that he is in the act of playing Commodore of the Yacht Club, Joseph Goebbels, Robert Mitchum, Maverick, Savonarola, the nice prep-school kid next door, and the snows of yesteryear."[1] As improbable as it may seem in our insistently middle-brow, image-conscious culture, the man thus playfully described has helped to alter the course of American politics.

More than any other individual, Buckley has made American conservatism an intellectually respectable political philosophy. By the sheer force of his personality and the depth of his commitment, he has fashioned a potent coalition from a dispirited group of militant anti-Communists, economic anarchists, and moss-backed traditionalists. Although millions know him as perhaps the most articulate—and certainly the most polysyllabic—spokesman for the American Right, he has advocated decriminalizing such activities as marijuana possession, prostitution, and private deviance; has argued for the ratification of the Panama Canal treaties; and has supported the election of new leftist Allard Lowenstein to the United States Congress. He has so infuriated certain segments of the Right that the late Ayn Rand used to leave any room he entered and Lyndon H. LaRouche has written an entire book on *How to Defeat Liberalism and William F. Buckley.* Nevertheless, his influence among respectable conservatives is such that in a single editorial Buckley discredited the John Birch Society and its eccentric leader Robert Welch. (No less an authority than Richard Nixon argues that he is the only man in America who could have accomplished that feat.)

Bill Buckley is a gadfly and a dilettante who practices a conservative version of the politics of joy. During three decades as a national presence, he has moved from the fringes of politics to the center of power. And perhaps no commentary more amusingly epitomizes his attitude toward his future role than one which appeared in the magazine he edits shortly after the 1980 votes were in: "With the election of Ronald Reagan, *National Review* assumes a new importance in American life. We become, as it were, an establishment organ; and we feel it only appropriate to alter our demeanor accordingly. This is therefore the last issue in which we shall indulge in levity. Connoisseurs of humor will have to get their yuks elsewhere. We have a nation to run."[2]

Boola Boola

William Frank Buckley, Jr. was born on November 24, 1925 to an iron-willed oil speculator and his gentle Southern wife. About this event, Dan Wakefield writes: "Though most men whose lives are devoted to a mission seem to follow the pattern of Paul, who had to wait until manhood for his revelation on the road to Damascus, William F. Buckley, Jr. seems to have had his vision at birth. If he had cried upon entering the world, one feels it would not have been in confusion or fear, but in an attempt to warn the doctors of the dangers of socialized medicine."[3]

Because the Buckley family was large (ten children), Irish-Catholic, and intensely political, inevitable comparisons have been made between it and the Kennedy clan.[4] Among the more perceptive of such comparisons are those of L. Clayton Dubois in commenting on the two patriarchs, Joe Kennedy and Will Buckley. According to Dubois:

> The fundamental difference between the visions of these men, it seems, is that Kennedy was convinced he deserved to be accepted by society and that one of his children, if not he himself, would offer the final proof by becoming President. With the same fierce pride, Buckley was convinced that society was not deserving of acceptance and that his children, who had no need to prove anything to anyone, should merely be right. So Kennedy set about mastering the compromises of public life, while Buckley spent much energy railing against them. His children would always stand on "principle."[5]

Like the mythical Pygmalion, Will Buckley may have succeeded too well in molding the personality of his Galatea. At the age of six, young Billie wrote to the King of England demanding repayment of that country's war debt. And, at the age of ten, two days after his matriculation at an exclusive British prep school, he called on the school's president to inform him of the deficiencies of the place. Finally, at the age of fifteen, "the young Mahster"—as he was known to his siblings—

received a memo from Father Buckley admonishing him "to be more moderate in the expression of your views and [to] try to express them in a way that would give as little offense as possible." As Larry L. King notes: "That must have been the most wasted advice since the Prime Minister counseled Edward VIII against hanging out with divorcees."[6]

After gleaning what learning he could from private tutors and prep schools, Bill Buckley enrolled in the University of Mexico. (It was now over twenty years since Will Buckley had been exiled from Mexico for backing the wrong dictator.) Young Buckley's studies were interrupted, however, by World War II and service to his country as a second lieutenant in the U.S. infantry. It is reliably reported that he had been on a San Antonio army base for less than forty-eight hours when he wrote the commanding general "telling him that he found a great waste of manpower, that his staff was inadequate, and expressed surprise that such things could be." Ever helpful, Buckley also submitted his own plan for redesigning the entire system. Fortunately, an intermediary persuaded Buckley not to send the letter and may well have spared him a court-martial for insubordination.[7]

Upon discharge from the army in 1946, Lieutenant Buckley entered Yale. (The freshman class that year was twice its normal size because the school had agreed to admit all those who had been accepted in previous years but had gone off to war.) It was there that Buckley met a young navy man from Omaha named L. Brent Bozell. The two would take Yale by storm.

Garry Wills tells us that Bozell "had won his college scholarship by high school oratory, and was eloquent for liberal causes. He soon led the campus chapter of United World Federalists—and got into trouble with the New Haven SPCA when he put tiny turtles in freshman mailboxes: The slogan stuck on each turtle's back said, "Hurry World Government."[8] And yet, even in those days, Bozell was flirting with both Catholicism and anti-Communism, and became committed to both under the influence of Bill Buckley. He was later to marry Bill's sister Patricia and to collaborate with Bill on *McCarthy and His Enemies,* a book which Wills derisively characterizes as "collected debate cards."

Another Buckley cohort at Yale was a brilliant and irascible political science professor named Willmoore Kendall. "His pugnacity and panache attracted Bill and Brent," Wills writes. "They made a formidable trio—all three bright, handsome, Catholic (in varying degrees), Spanish-speaking war veterans, glib, argumentative."[9] A "learned hick" from Oklahoma who carried within his difficult personality a strain of Midwest populism, Kendall seemed to take outrageous positions largely for the pleasure of scandalizing the genteel liberalism of Yale. (He was later to be immortalized as Willis Mosby in Saul Bellow's *Mosby's Memoirs.*) Wills contends that much of Bill Buckley's syntax derives directly from his exposure to Kendall. "I had thought everyone talked like Bill at *National Review,*" he writes. "But they were talking like Willmoore—like the Oklahoma boy whose diction had been sharpened by his years at Oxford and his doctoral studies in Romance languages."[10]

Although something of a young-Turk polemicist, Buckley could be gracious and endearing in private.[11] Even men like philosophy professor Paul Weiss and fellow student William Sloane Coffin, who frequently disagreed with Buckley, found him a personable young man. "He was a charming human being—and still is," says Weiss. "Remarkably courteous and civilised, he was a polite, considerate, and thoughtful host."[12] It is also a matter of record that Buckley made his acceptance of membership in the Fence, a Yale fraternity, contingent upon its accepting his roommate, Thomas H. Guinzberg (who was later to become president of Viking Press). At that time, the social life of Yale was not particularly hospitable to Jews and had only recently begun to accommodate itself to Catholics. Thus, Buckley's stance was both principled and courageous.

Bill Buckley began his career as a political journalist during the year that he served as chairman of Yale's student newspaper the *Daily News.* (Intent on winning that position, which is decided by vote of the paper's staff, he asked his brother Jim if it would be ethical to vote for himself. Upon Jim's advice, he proceeded to do so and was somewhat embarrassed to be elected unanimously.) As one might expect, his tenure was marked by outspoken editorials that were conservative, pro-Christian, and anti-Communist. In fact, these editorials stirred such controversy that Paul Weiss "thought Bill an unwitting forerunner of campus dissidence and defiance of authority."[13] According to Francis Donahue, long-time paid advertising manager of the *Daily News:* "I never worked with a more considerate or fairer man. He would cut anything out of the *News* to make room for arguments against him [self]."[14]

Apparently, the student newspaper was a social as well as a journalistic institution. Prospective staff members would "heel" for the paper much as prospective fraternity members would "pledge" those organizations. When Buckley was chairman of the *News,* he held the annual heeler's party in his campus suite. Of the twenty-seven apprentices attending, only eleven would be selected for the staff. The custom was to get everyone drunk before the announcements were made, and, to that end, Tom Guinzburg poured twenty-seven bottles of gin into a barrel and added one bottle of vermouth. "After a half-hour of chug-a-lugging," Buckley recalls, "a great raucous was born, and presently the telephone rang. The College Master—demanding the immediate evacuation of my quarters."[15] In an effort to comply, Bill called a local restaurateur named Charley, ordered fifty-four hamburgers, and sought to organize his crew for a dignified withdrawal.

The best-laid plan immediately went awry when the lad at the head of the line promptly collapsed outside Buckley's room, "a plastic smile smeared over his angelic face" (*CS,* 223). At that moment, the weekly full-dress fellows parade issued forth from the master's suite next door. The goodly gentlemen were thus forced to step over "the corpse of our immobilized heeler, the personification of Innocence Traduced at Yale." At the head of the parade was Thornton Wilder, "who had first to step over the body." (Buckley remembers his smiling "urbanely at me and Tom, as if he had negotiated a mud puddle" [*CS,* 222].) To make matters worse, when they arrived at the restaurant *all twenty-seven* of Buckley's charges began throwing up, a development which did little for the reputation of Charley's cuisine. But tradition had been maintained. (Returning to Charley's nearly twenty years later, Buckley recalls a mishap from his own freshman heeler's party: "We were forced to chug-a-lug, and midway through one such ordeal I keeled over and hit a table on my way down. I woke up in the hospital."[16])

In 1950, Bill Buckley was graduated from Yale with honors. Selected to give that year's Alumni Day address, he composed an indictment of the liberalism and secularism of his alma mater. Then, in what was perhaps the most counterproductive move since a South African official threw Mohandas K. Gandhi out of a segregated railway car, the Yale authorities suppressed the speech. Undaunted, Buckley simply launched his polemical career with *God and Man at Yale.*

Forward Into Battle

During his three decades in public life, William Buckley has become a recognizable persona. In the flesh, he cuts an unmistakable figure:

His hair is greying (and needs cutting); his skin is weathered, a sailor's. He has, even in clothes newly pressed, a permanently rumpled air. He hunches his shoulders, writhes in his clothes, jams his hands in his back pockets, forcing the pants ever lower on his hips and his shirttail out. Gesturing, he spreads his fingers so taut they seem bent back; a slim ballpoint pen (red ink) is always wedged between the fingers of his right hand (or locked to its palm with his thumb). . . . [He] speaks so low that staccato clearings of his throat seem explosive. He has the English way of groping elegantly for a word and stuttering to a climax.[17]

In the early 1950s, however, such familiarity was yet to come.

Newly graduated from Yale and a controversial author, Buckley spent several months in Mexico as a CIA agent. He returned to the United States in 1952 and served briefly as associate editor of the *American Mercury,* a once formidable journal which had gone steadily downhill since the glory days of H. L. Mencken and George Jean Nathan. This experience, among others, helped to convince him of the need for a national publication to articulate conservative opinion in a respectable and literate format. In 1955, *National Review* was founded for that very purpose.

In its early days, *NR* was something of a snakepit of sectarian controversy. Because the "conservative movement" itself was at best a loose coalition of antileftists who professed very different visions of the good society, it required a massive ecumenical effort on Buckley's part to hold that coalition together. "When I went there," writes Garry Wills, "[*NR*] was not yet two years old. It was Bill's whole life, consuming his extraordinary energies. . . . A cranky band of bright editors taxed Bill's energy, fighting the world and each other, trying to use or help Bill, each intent on steering this new bark off in his own direction. . . . Bill tried to stay above the conflict, half ignoring, half downplaying it. He alone was more intent on saving the ship than on steering it."[18] Although there were those who fell by the wayside, others rose to take their place. Now over twenty-five years old, *NR* has not only endured, but—with the election of Ronald Reagan—has prevailed.

While trying to keep peace among the older men on his editorial board, Buckley was also busy recruiting talented but untested younger writers. In addition to Wills, others who wrote for *NR* early in their careers include John Leonard, Joan Didion, Arlene Croce, Renata Adler, Guy Davenport, George F. Will, and D. Keith Mano. The fact that each of these individuals has since established a reputation in the world of letters suggests that not the least of Buckley's virtues is his prescience as a literary patron.

The appearance of *National Review* did not go unnoticed by the liberal opposition. Like the neighborhood bully intent on putting the smart aleck new kid on the block in his place, the big guns of the liberal establishment came out smoking against *NR* and its cheeky editor. Perhaps the most notorious of the attacks was Dwight MacDonald's "Scrambled Eggheads on the Right."[19]

Fuming against what he considered a sophomoric brand of conservatism, MacDonald charged Buckley's magazine with the sins of "opacity," "brutality," "banality," and "vulgarity." "Here are the ideas, here is the style of the *lumpen* bourgeoisie," he writes, "the half-educated provincials . . . who responded to Huey Long, Father Coughlin, and Senator McCarthy." To his mind the editors of *NR* were "men from the underground, the intellectually underprivileged."[20] Special invective, however, was reserved for the chief underground man: "Had [Buckley] been born a generation earlier, he would have been making the cafeterias of 14th Street ring with Marxian dialectics. He is a lively and engaging fellow, and would make an excellent journalist if he had a little more humor, common sense, and intellectual curiosity; also if he knew how to write. The tongue is his instrument of expression, not the typewriter."[21]

At the same time that he was developing a public reputation, Buckley also was establishing a home with his wife Patricia and son Christopher. A couple of years after their marriage in 1950, Bill and Pat Buckley moved from an apartment building in New York (where Marilyn Monroe was one of their fellow tenants) to a seaside house in Stamford, Connecticut. Buckley made a downpayment of $65,000 (he would later take out a $25,000 mortgage at an unheard of interest rate of 4⅜ percent, which was "twice the highest rate recommended by Lord Keynes")[22] and joined the landed gentry.

In his amusing and affectionate essay "The House," Buckley insists that he loves this dwelling in spite of, perhaps even because of, his wife's periodic decorating frenzies. He tells us that "the sun room soon became the bordello the Shah couldn't afford. Then the living room, a kind of Haitian concentrate" (*H,* 404). From his own special domain—"a music room, featuring a beautiful harpsichord and the worst keyboard artist since Harry Truman" (*H,* 404)—Buckley is able to view Long Island Sound and "framing the garden, a slender treetrunk trained like a geisha girl from childhood to give pleasure" (*H,* 405). "There, in the winter, the fireplace alight, a proper musician performing live or on record, you can see what the pilgrims saw, as if under glass, and understand the compulsion to Thanksgiving" (*H,* 405).

Although Mrs. Buckley is not in the public eye as much as the wives of many other famous men, she does play a significant role in her husband's autobiographical writings (particularly in his sailing memoir *Airborne*).

She is a native of Vancouver, Canada, an Anglican, and a former Vassar classmate of Bill's *sister* Patricia. (The future Mrs. L. Brent Bozell is quoted as saying of her classmate: "Pat looks like a queen, she acts like a queen, and is just the wife for Billy."[23]) By all accounts, their life together has been both happy and decorous.

Far from being an all-American sportsman, Bill Buckley seems devoted to only two recreational pastimes—sailing and skiing. For a while during his youth, however, these enthusiasms shared a place in his heart with flying. As a freshman at Yale, he and five partners purchased an Ercoupe called *Alexander's Horse* and began surreptitiously to pursue a sport which, in 1946, their fathers regarded as nothing more "than rank technological presumption fit only for daredevils" (*H,* 454).

After breezing through his first couple of lessons, Buckley became convinced that there was nothing to flying. So, when he encountered a friend who needed desperately to get to Boston for a dinner with his inamorata, Buckley found himself saying "as though I were P. G. Wodehouse himself, 'Why my dear friend, grieve no more. I shall fly you to Boston'" (*H,* 456). The trip up was uneventful, in that Buckley's friend, who had been a pilot during the war, was at the controls. On the way back, however, young Bill was soloing for the first time. Since he had not yet been instructed on the use of his radio, he thought nothing of the fact that he was tuned in to a soap opera rather than a control tower. Also, since he had neglected to account for the switch from daylight saving to standard time, the sun went down an hour earlier than he had expected. By the time he reached New Haven, he was flying 100 feet off the ground.

Another harrowing experience occurred when all of Buckley's exams were crammed into the first two days of a five-day exam period. When the last of these tests was over, he felt giddy with fatigue, elation, and benzedrine. So, naturally, he decided to take a spin in *Alexander's Horse.* He zoomed off by himself, heading toward downtown New Haven, climbing to 4,000 feet. "There," he tells us, "I fell asleep" (*H,* 459). Fortunately, even though his body was crashing, he managed to summon sufficient adrenelin to keep his plane from following suit.

The final flight of *Alexander's Horse* transpired when Buckley decided that he must take Brent Bozell to the Ethel Walker School to see Maureen, the only one of the Buckley siblings who had yet to meet their future brother-in-law. Armed with a crude map which Maureen had drawn, the young men flew to the school, where Brother Bill negotiated a difficult landing over "the tallest trees this side of the California redwoods" (*H,* 460). Flush with pride, Buckley landed, reduced his speed to thirty miles per hour, and promptly ran into a drainage ditch which Maureen had neglected to indicate on her map. Since the repair bills for the plane would have been exactly equal to what the boys had originally paid for it, *Alexander's Horse* was put out of its misery, its carcass going for $100. "Father was right, as usual," Buckley concludes. "I couldn't afford to fly" (*H,* 462).

If aviation was not Buckley's forte, polemicism clearly was. While the left was running roughshod through the 1960s, Buckley was gaining increasing stature as a visible and vocal force for the political right. In 1960, he helped to organize Young Americans for Freedom, a conservative youth group which would outlive its more histrionic left-wing counterpart, Students for a Democratic Society. Then, in 1961, he was instrumental in founding the New York State Conservative Party, an organization whose banner he would carry unsuccessfully in the 1965 New York mayoral election. His personal stock was also rising with the inauguration of a weekly newspaper column in 1962 and its expansion to a thrice-weekly in 1964. Finally, in 1966, he hit the airwaves with a regular interview show called *Firing Line*. He had become that most unconservative of animals—a media personality.

Surveying the Buckley phenomenon in 1967, Larry L. King wrote: "He is an international traveler who is strong for states' rights; a Honda '50' hot-rock who plays the clavichord; in one moment a mixer-and-mingler with a Rotary Club grip and in the next a Grand Duke icily looking down his nose to accept the peasants' birthday bows. He is an author who sometimes sides with censors, and a celebrated intellectual who has spoken of 'the hoax of academic freedom'—a swinging Old Fogy who has become a legend in his time."[24]

Depressing Ubiquity

In his 1978 novel *Stained Glass,* Bill Buckley has his characters make sport of a well-known pundit named Old Razzia: "Himmelfarb drew himself up and delivered an imitation of the writer [Razzia], whose mannerisms were widely known, and widely caricatured, because of his depressing ubiquity: he was a syndicated columnist, a television host, an author, editor of his own magazine, and had now announced he would also write novels!"[25] Whether Buckley's own ubiquity is depressing or not is, of course, a matter of opinion. What cannot be gainsaid, however, is that by the end of the sixties he *was* practically everywhere. (Indeed, Irving Howe "sees Buckley as something fashionable to have around—

the way every salon or cocktail party in the 1920s and 1930s had its adopted Parlor Pink for amusement and diversion."[26]) At least everywhere that counted.

One such place was the grand ballroom of New York City's Plaza Hotel on November 28, 1966. There, Truman Capote threw a celebrated masked ball in honor of *Washington Post* publisher Kay Graham and invited 500 of his closest friends. "Depending on which masked and bejeweled guest was talking," reports *Life* magazine, "it was the party of the decade, the party of the century, or plainly it was the biggest and most glorious bash ever."[27] The guest list was nothing if not eclectic. Among the "jarring juxtapositions" noted by *Life* were: "Marianne Moore and Henry Geldzahler; Frank Sinatra and Alice Roosevelt Longworth; Janet Flanner and Andy Warhol; Henry Ford and Norman Mailer; McGeorge Bundy and Douglas Fairbanks; Walter Lippmann and Roddy McDowall; William Buckley and Lynda Bird Johnson" (*JE*, 270). A year after the event, the only jetset conservative in attendance recorded his observations in an essay entitled "The Politics of Truman Capote's Ball."

Essentially, Buckley argues, "the politics of Capote's ball was that there was no politics" (*JE*, 270); at least not in the partisan sense. (Although "Jerry Robbins wondered if we weren't the list of those to be shot first by the Red Guard [;] Kenneth Galbraith said no, not as long as *he* was on it" [*JE*, 271].) This fact greatly distressed Pete Hamill, who wrote a nasty review of the evening for the *New York Post*. Hamill's technique was "to contrive wisps of frivolous conversation, á la *The Women*, and juxtapose them with horror stories from the Vietnamese battlefront (get it?), so as to effect a Stendhalian contrast that would Arouse the Conscience of Versailles" (*JE*, 262). (After making the obvious comparison between this device and that of Carl Foreman's film *The Victors*, Buckley proceeds to make the equally obvious point that "if society accepted the dictum that so long as some people are suffering, others may not party together, there would never be any partying at all" [*JE*, 263].)

And yet, if we regard politics in its extrapartisan sense—as simply the effective control of groups of people—Capote's ball can be seen as a consummately political affair. The fact that such a heterogeneous group of people could come together and enjoy themselves to the point that they would be talking about the party a year later is a tribute to Capote's genius for human relations. That is one political assertion about which both William Buckley and Lynda Bird would surely agree.

The beautiful people who party with Truman Capote, however, do not constitute the only fast crowd with which Bill Buckley runs. He has actually been seen with Hugh Hefner at the Playboy mansion and once received a Christmas check from Hefner's magazine (a gratuity which he returned so as not to be considered part of the *Playboy* family). His association with America's foremost erotic monthly began when he was interviewed by the magazine in spring of 1970. He later accepted *Playboy*'s invitation to write a long article about his trip to the Soviet Union, calculating that he would thus reach 10 percent of the reading population of America. (Since he received only one letter about that article, it is questionable whether many people paused to admire his prose on their way to the centerfold. However, neither this experience nor any stuffed-shift moralistic scruples prevented him from writing about China for *Playboy* or allowing *Penthouse* to publish excerpts from *Marco Polo, If You Can.*)

One of Buckley's most fascinating characteristics is the obvious discontinuity between his conservative philosophy and his iconoclastic personality. He tells with evident relish the story of a New York editor for *Paris-Match* who entertained two of his countrymen by tuning in a *Firing Line* debate between Buckley and Hefner. "Inexplicably, the picture came on but the sound did not, until after four or five minutes, when finally the marginal twiddle with the dial brought it on, and the Frenchmen after a second or two winced with surprise because, studying the speechless visages of the principals, they had all tacitly come to the conclusion that I was Hefner, and Hefner was I; he being, in the reading of our faces, clearly the conservative ascetic, I the freeliver" (*CS,* 64–65).[28]

If the 1960s were years of left-wing ascendency, the seventies saw the pendulum moving back toward the right. The decade began with the swearing in of James Buckley as junior Senator from New York (running on the Conservative Party ticket, he had won a plurality in a three-way race against a Democrat and a liberal Republican) and ended with the election of Ronald Reagan to the presidency (never mind that Watergate and Carter also occurred during the decade). Bill Buckley got his first taste of public office by serving on the advisory committee for the United States Information Agency and as a member of the U.S. Delegation to the United Nations. More important, he published a book a year—including his first three novels.

One of the mixed blessings of being a media star and best-selling author is the obligatory tour of the talk-show circuit. Although appearances with Johnny, Merv, and company enable a writer to sell both himself and his views, they also tend to reduce one to the level of a literate Zsa Zsa Gabor. In an effort to resist "that commingling that can transform an appearance on a talk show into a prolonged nightmare," Buckley has at least contrived in recent years to appear, perform, and depart. "During my youth," he tells us, "promoting my books on the old Dave Garroway 'Today' show, I once found myself thinking of J. Fred Muggs [a trained monkey who was a regular on the show] as probably my closest friend" (*H*, 324).

Perhaps the time that he felt most foolish was when he was cajoled into appearing on the Dinah Shore show. The problem was that Dinah's guests were required to perform at their hobby. For Buckley, this meant playing the harpsichord, an instrument which "cannot be made to sound, at the hands of an amateur, endearing—like Jack Benny's violin" (*H*, 324). The only thing that sustained him as he muddled through was the thought that in his entire life he had never known anyone who had ever seen the Dinah Shore show. (Nothing against Dinah, but Bill Buckley does not ordinarily associate with daytime television buffs.)

A couple of weeks later, Buckley and a friend landed in a small private plane on an airstrip east of New Orleans. This was to be Buckley's first meeting with a man whom he considers to be his hero—the distinguished novelist and philosopher Walker Percy. As the travelers were pulling up to the terminal, "a tall lanky man in Levis approached the airplane and, as [Buckley] emerged from it, shot out his hand. 'I'm Walker Percy, Mr. Buckley. I feel I know you. Just saw you on the Dinah Shore show'" (*H*, 325).

On December 5, 1980, the friends of *National Review* gathered in the grand ballroom of the Plaza Hotel to celebrate the twenty-fifth anniversary of that journal's founding. The guest list included such luminaries as Murray Kempton, New York State Senator-elect Alphonse D'Amato, Rosalyn Tureck, New York City Mayor Ed Koch, Henry Kissinger, Clare Booth Luce, William Casey, Walter Cronkite, and Tom Wolfe. (His keepers had the president-elect scheduled elsewhere that evening.) Savoring the results of the recent election and contemplating the progress made by the conservative movement during the previous quarter-century, George Will declared: "And before there was Ronald Reagan there was Barry Goldwater, and before there was Barry Goldwater there was *National Review*, and before there was *National Review* there was Bill Buckley with a spark in his mind. . . ."[29]

Chapter Two

Chairman Bill

Many observers question whether contemporary American conservatism is—in fact—contemporary, American, or conservative. No doubt, part of the problem lies in the fact that conservatism became a political movement before it had an articulated body of thought. For this reason, the present-day right has devoted considerable intellectual man hours to the attempt to understand itself. One can therefore appreciate William Buckley's consternation when he is asked on the lecture circuit to define conservatism, "preferably in one sentence." His usual response to such a query is to quote Richard Weaver's statement that conservatism "is a paradigm of essences towards which the phenomenology of the world is in continuing approximation."[1] But then, as Louis Armstrong once said of jazz: people who have to ask what it is wouldn't understand if you told them.

A House of Many Mansions

George H. Nash and others have noted that the brand of conservatism expounded in *National Review* is not so much a single party line as a coalition of three distinct philosophies united by a common enemy on the left.[2] Accordingly, much of what passes for conservative apologetics—particularly in Buckley's writings—is little more than an attack on liberalism.[3] One might even argue that if liberalism did not exist, the conservative "movement" would fragment into hostile camps. Indeed, in the period since World War II, that movement has rarely been free of factional strife.

One element of the conservative coalition consists of economic libertarians—advocates of the free market who agree with Thoreau's contention that "that government is best which governs not at all." However, substantial terminological confusion arises from the fact that

in the nineteenth century proponents of laissez-faire were generally referred to as "liberals." Thus, as twentieth-century liberalism became
synonymous with the welfare state, adherents to the older liberal tradition
found themselves part of the political right.

Although libertarians trace their roots back to Adam Smith, much of
the impetus for their current revival comes from the work of two
Austrian economists—Ludwig von Mises and Friedrich A. Hayek. Of
particular importance is Hayek's 1944 classic *The Road to Serfdom*. An
enormously popular book written primarily for the layman, Hayek's
tome inspired heated controversy in Britain and America at a time when
collectivism seemed to be the wave of the future for both democratic and
totalitarian countries.[4] Meanwhile, the libertarian gospel was being
spread in the United States by evangelists like John Chamberlain, Henry
Hazlitt, and Frank Chodorov writing in such journals as the *Freeman*.[5]

If libertarians were forced into the conservative camp by historical
circumstance, cultural traditionalists had been there all along. While
sharing the libertarians' concern for individual freedom, limited government, and private property, the traditionalists also recognized the
socially disruptive effects of corporate capitalism. Consequently, they
tended to be more interested in preserving the continuity of inherited
religious and cultural values—of what Russell Kirk calls the "permanent
things"—than in preaching the virtues of an atomistic economic system.

The intellectual genealogy of the traditionalist movement is suggested by the subtitle of Russell Kirk's *The Conservative Mind—From Burke
to Eliot*. This subtitle also suggests one of the difficulties which traditionalist conservatism has had to confront—the lack of an indigenously American matrix. Historically, America has been a liberal and
progressive nation which has been inhospitable to Tory sentiment. Only
in the South has this country had anything resembling an hierarchical
social order. Hence, the antecedents of contemporary American traditionalism are disproportionately Southern.[6] One can trace a line of
descent from John Randolph of Roanoke through John C. Calhoun to the
Nashville Agrarians. Not surprisingly, Richard Weaver—whose *Ideas
Have Consequences* (1948) is something of a sacred text among
traditionalists—studied under the Agrarians while doing graduate work
in English at Vanderbilt.

Joining the libertarians and the traditionalists was an odd assortment
of ex-radicals—Whittaker Chambers, James Burnham, Max Eastman,
and others—who had been converted to a kind of messianic anti-
Communism. Essentially a negative and combative philosophy, anti-

Communism offered no positive vision of society (for that its adherents had to look elsewhere). Instead, its primary concern was with defeating the Communist enemy both at home and abroad. The fact that James Burnham's *National Review* column was entitled "The Third World War" says a great deal about the apocalyptic terms in which conservatives viewed America's struggle against the "Red Menace."

Because of its insistently pragmatic character, anti-Communism occasionally came into conflict with the more rigidly principled libertarian and traditionalist movements. For example, many libertarians believed that Communism posed less of a threat to American freedom than did the huge increase in government power which was needed to wage the Cold War. Similarly, traditionalists tended to be appalled by the ruthless tactics of anti-Communist folk hero Joseph McCarthy. Whatever else he may have been, Tail-Gunner Joe was no Tory gentleman.

As the loyal son of a Roman Catholic capitalist, Bill Buckley is a natural-born libertarian and traditionalist (a fact which may account for his rather bizarre equation of Christianity and free enterprise in *God and Man at Yale*). If his zeal to rid the world of tyranny is more of an acquired taste (he was isolationist prior to World War II), Buckley has nevertheless shown the typical convert's enthusiasm by siding with the anti-Communists in most of their disputes with the other two wings of the conservative coalition. When the libertarians and the traditionalists have gone after each other, however, he has tried to steer a middle course—paying homage to both the dynamo and the Virgin.

One is tempted, therefore, to see Buckley as a general who mediates disputes among his troops so as to keep them mobilized for the battle against the greater foe. But such a characterization tells only part of the story. It seems to me that Buckley's political significance cannot be explained solely in strategic or even philosophical terms. Instead, his most important contributions to the conservative movement may well be aesthetic and psychological. At a time when much of the American Right saw itself as a minority doomed to failure, Buckley was prescient enough and bold enough to suspect that conservatism might be a once and future faith.

A World to Win

In 1956, William Buckley said that he would sooner be governed by the first 2,000 names in the Boston telephone directory than by the 2,000 members of the Harvard faculty. The impishly populist tone of this statement clearly reflects the influence of his old mentor from Yale, Willmoore Kendall. (One can also detect Kendall's influence in the authoritarian cadences of Buckley's *God and Man at Yale* [1951] and *McCarthy and His Enemies* [1954].) Although we will examine both books in detail later on, it is worth noting that Buckley's early reputation was as an eloquent apostle of intolerance.

At a time when conservatives of both the libertarian and traditionalist persuasions advocated natural-rights theories, Kendall declared himself a majority-rule democrat. He bitterly distrusted the notion of an open society and argued that the majority had both the right and the duty to suppress dissent. He applauded the defenders of social hegemony from the prosecutors of Socrates to Senator Joseph McCarthy, and declared that the true American tradition was "not 'preferred freedoms' but 'riding somebody out of town on a rail.' "[7]

Of course, the Buckley-Kendall position involves a considerable gamble. If those who formulate and enforce the official orthodoxy are knaves or fools, it is the virtuous and wise who will suffer.[8] To entrust the role of Grand Inquisitor to an electoral majority, or to the first 2,000 names in the Boston phone book, is an awesome act of faith. Kendall, however, believed in the native good sense of the American people. As long as they were accurately informed about the issues confronting them, the people could be counted on to respond wisely. It was necessary only to assure that they had enough light to find their own way. Shedding this light was the vocation to which Kendall's disciple William Buckley dedicated himself.

In terms of their sheer variety and scope, Buckley's writings would seem to constitute a conservative *summa*. And yet, what he has produced is more polemics than philosophy. One is apt to come away from this body of work perplexed about what conservatism is, but certain about what it is not. The essay "Notes Toward an Empirical Definition of Conservatism"—the bulk of which is devoted to an account of feuds between *National Review* and various ideologues of the far right—is an excellent case in point.

From its very inception, *National Review* has had to guard against extremists who would shatter the conservative coalition by pushing it too far in a single direction. The first such threat came from the libertarian camp in the person of Ayn Rand. (Upon first meeting him, Rand looked Buckley square in the eyes and said, "You ahrr too intelligent to beleef in Gott!"; about which comment Wilfrid Sheed remarked: "Well, that is an ice-breaker" [*CS*, 147].) Exalting the jungle ethic of survival and what she calls the "virtue of selfishness," Rand constructs a kind of atheistic metaphysic around technological progress and human greed. As Whittaker Chambers notes in his review of her novel *Atlas Shrugged:* "Randian Man, like Marxian Man, is made the center of a godless world" (*JE,* 14).

After dispensing with Ayn Rand, Buckley's essay turns its attention to other, more benign, advocates of laissez-faire who have managed to get themselves banished from the *National Review* fold. Foremost among these is the economist Murray Rothbard. Although Buckley finds Rothbard's eccentric right-wing anarchism to be intellectually stimulating, he does not think that there is much practical benefit to be derived from discussing alternatives to municipalized streets. More troublesome, however, is the anti-anti-Communism of the Rothbard libertarians. These men, according to Buckley, "wish to *live* their fanatical antistatism, and the result is a collision between the basic policies they urge and those urged by conservatives who recognize that the state sometimes is, and is today as never before, the necessary instrument of our proximate deliverance" (*JE,* 17).

To be sure, the anti-Communists themselves can go to dangerous extremes. For Buckley, the prime offenders in this regard are Robert Welch and the John Birch Society. Welch's primary error, in Buckley's view, is his assumption that "one may reliably infer subjective motivation from objective result" (*JE,* 19). According to such a view, the geopolitical setbacks of the West afford tangible proof that our national leaders are actually enemy agents. Indeed, Welch has gone so far as to accuse Dwight Eisenhower of being a Communist—a charge which Buckley dismisses with Russell Kirk's famous retort: "Eisenhower isn't a Communist—he is a golfer" (*JE,* 19).

In the interest of symmetry, Buckley probably should have concluded his essay with a discussion of some egregious case of *traditionalist* extremism. Although no flagrant examples of such may have been at hand in the early 1960s, one would strike very close to home by the end of the decade. Throughout the sixties, Buckley's brother-in-law and early colleague L. Brent Bozell became an increasingly militant Catholic theocrat.

Clad in purple berets and brandishing wooden crosses, Bozell's Sons of Thunder[9] committed civil disobedience at abortion clinics. When not engaged in such direct action, they contemplated the nature of a Christian social order in *Triumph* magazine. (While other conservatives cheered the prosecution of the Fathers Berrigan, *Triumph* argued that clerics ought not to be subject to the secular law, and should be tried—if at all—by an ecclesiastical tribunal.) As a young man whom Buckley quotes in *Cruising Speed* ruefully observes: *"Triumph* is . . . as hostile to the American ethos as any revolutionary organ on the hard Left" (*CS,* 236).

Sectarian squabbles on the right, however, are mere skirmishes when compared to Buckley's crusade against the forces of liberalism. Indeed, his third book—appropriately titled *Up From Liberalism* (1959)—is devoted exclusively to that crusade. Although probably most memorable for its entertaining exposure of liberal hypocrisy and fatuousness, *Up From Liberalism* is also useful for the light it sheds on its author's own basic philosophy.

One of the fundamental objections which Buckley raises to liberal ideology is that it is rooted in epistemological relativism, a habit of mind which stresses method at the expense of substance. "Method is king," he writes, "—because things are 'real' only in proportion as they are discoverable by the scientific method; with the result that method logically directs all intellectual (to which we now subordinate moral and metaphysical) traffic."[10] One of the most glaring examples of this preoccupation with method is the liberal's "obsessive, even fetishistic" commitment to democracy.

Although it may seem strange to hear one who studied at the feet of Willmoore Kendall say disparaging things about democracy, we must keep in mind the limited sense in which Buckley is using the term. It is not democracy's encouragement of social conformity which Buckley finds objectionable, but rather the liberal's attempt to use democracy to promote economic and political equality.

One searches *Up From Liberalism* in vain to find the eloquent contempt for mob rule which informs Thoreau's "Essay on Civil Disobedience." Or much solicitude for minority rights and civil liberties as those concepts are generally understood. When Buckley contrasts democracy and freedom, he is not championing the right of political dissent so much as he is defending the free market against governmental encroachments.

It is not difficult to see how a categorical allegiance to democracy tends toward the promotion of socialism. If a representative government is merely an institutional expression of the people's will, then an increase in governmental power is—by definition—an increase in the peoples' control over their collective destiny. The welfare state is thus the perfect embodiment of utilitarian democracy. Buckley, however, advocates a society in which "*the people would cherish a self denying ordinance under which they would never use their political power in such fashion as to diminish the area of human freedom*. That is to say, in an ideally free society, the use of one's political freedom would be highly restricted" (*UL,* 123).

At the time that *Up From Liberalism* was being written, one of the most palpable restrictions of political freedom was the non-enfranchisement of Negro voters in the South. While liberal proponents of absolute democracy found this situation to be morally abhorrent, conservatives were far more tolerant. "If the majority wills what is socially atavistic," Buckley writes, "then to thwart the majority may be the indicated, though concededly the undemocratic, course. It is more important for a community, wherever situated geographically, to affirm and live by civilized standards than to labor at the job of swelling the voting lists" (*UL,* 128). (Later on, he identifies integrated education and social welfare as the two forms of social atavism which Negro voters would most likely inflict upon their more civilized white brethren.)

It seems to me that Buckley's attack on democracy misfires because his arguments against extension of the franchise go too far, while his defense of individual freedom does not go far enough. It is one thing to advocate a little white paternalism for some of the cannibal democracies of Africa; it is quite another to imply that there is no essential difference between, say, Idi Amin and the National Association for the Advancement of Colored People. Welfare-state liberals may be wrong-headed without necessarily being socially atavistic. By seeking to restrict their political rights, Buckley is simply cutting the moral ground out from under his otherwise compelling defense of economic freedom.

At a more fundamental level, Buckley finds the liberal faith to be spiritually deficient. He sees the liberal millenium as "the state in which a citizen divides his day equally between pulling levers in voting booths (Voting for what? It does not matter; what matters is that he vote); writing dissenting letters to the newspapers (Dissenting from what? It does not matter; just so he dissents); and eating (Eating what? It does not matter, though one should wash the food down with fluoridated water)" (*UL,* 155). Herein lies the ultimate failure of an instrumentalist political creed: it "has no eschatology; no vision, no fulfillment, no point of arrival" (*UL,* 111). Artistically, this is a truly withering critique. However, it is one which relies on specious generalizations.

In creating a demonology of liberalism, Buckley cannot have it both ways. The liberal cannot simultaneously be a dangerous ideologue and an ineffectual dilettante. The problem may lie in the fact that liberals do not endorse Buckley's Falangist linking of right-wing politics and Christianity. It is certainly possible to be stirred to sacrifice by a *secular* political commitment. At least in the United States, the labor and civil rights movements have produced more martyrs than conservatism has. If the genteel version of liberalism is an effete faith, the fault is in its genteelness not in its liberalism.

Moreover, to say that there is no distinctively liberal eschatology is not quite the same thing as saying that no liberal has an eschatology. Empirically, we know that there are large numbers of people who are both Christian and liberal. These people may be mistaken, even schizophrenic, but their very existence belies the notion that the conflict between right and left is between Christian and infidel. Indeed, Buckley has never hesitated to make common cause with non-Christian libertarians. Max Eastman and *National Review* did not part company because it wouldn't tolerate his atheism, but because he couldn't abide its piety.

Suppose, however, we concede that liberalism *qua* liberalism is more concerned with temporal method than with eternal substance? Much the same thing might be said about Buckley's brief for the free market (is capitalism itself not a methodology?). Some would even contend that while freedom is a higher political end than democracy, it is not the highest goal of civilization. For example, Brent Bozell argues that "the chief purpose of politics is to aid the quest for virtue." Political and economic freedom is, at best, only a partial means toward that end. "The story of how the free society has come to take priority over the good society," Bozell writes, "is the story of the decline of the West."[11]

Of course, it is possible to junk the theocratic model altogether and argue that eschatology is not the proper concern of a *political* philosophy. The best that we can hope to accomplish in the secular world of politics must inevitably fall short of realizing the Kingdom of God. To concentrate on the means for promoting social harmony rather than on the substance of a millenial dream may be more the mark of a realist than of a fetishist.

Nor is a reluctance to sacrilize politics necessarily a liberal characteristic. In his 1961 essay "The Convenient State" (which is still the initial entry in the Buckley-edited anthology *Did You Ever See a Dream Walking?*),[12] Garry Wills maintains—on conservative grounds—that the political realm is not an appropriate context for pursuing theological ends. Although the state—like any other institution—is bound by the laws of morality and justice, it is not the specific function of government to enforce morality and justice as such. Instead, the state's role is the more modest and limited one of achieving consensus—and, hence, peace—within a society. As Saint Augustine observed: "A people is a gathering of many rational individuals united by accord on loved things held in common."[13]

The political process, then, is largely a people's attempt to define itself, to identify those loved things which it holds in common. By faulting liberalism for its excessive celebration of this process, Buckley is accusing the left of being too timid, too cautious, indeed, too conservative. What he is attempting is nothing less than a radical reversal of ideological stereotypes. It turns out that we only thought that liberals were schematic visionaries. In reality, they are unimaginative formalists, while conservatives are the true utopians. Or so Buckley would have us believe.

To mount such an ingenious attack on liberalism requires an intellectual daring which some might find incompatible with the conservative virtues of prudence and predictability. And yet, William Buckley fascinates precisely because his message and his style seem so frequently to clash. Is he, in fact, a "true conservative"? "I feel I qualify spiritually and philosophically," he writes; "but temperamentally I am not of the breed" (*JE,* 12).

Chapter Three
Coldpolitik

When asked in a 1970 interview to identify the most significant "event or development" of the previous decade, William Buckley replied: "The philosophical acceptance of coexistence by the West."[1] A military acceptance of the Communist empire, he argues, is understandable; but a moralistic power such as the United States loses part of its legitimacy by becoming too complacent about the fact of the Iron Curtain. Indeed, during that Golden Age known as the Cold War 50s, it was the mark of a liberal to want to "contain" Communism, while the conservative was apt to urge outright liberation of the East. In the years since the fifties, however, the terms of that dialogue have shifted radically in the direction of what used to be called appeasement.

That the old liberal doctrine of containment has come to be regarded as "neo-conservative" (and the old right-wing passion for liberation as neo-lunacy) is surely an historical transformation of considerable moment. And yet, if we extend our perspective back far enough, it is interesting to note that the pre–Cold War foreign policy of conservatism was based on an earlier form of coexistence called isolationism. Even though traditionalists and libertarians have never been congenial to the formulations of Marx and Lenin, and despite the fact that Attorney General A. Mitchell Palmer deported some "reds" in the early 1920s, aggressive anti-Communism is largely a post–World War II addition to conservative thought. To be sure, the imperialism of Stalin and the treachery of Alger Hiss were the most important factors in shattering isolationist sentiment on the right; however, the actual forging of a conservative anti-Communist consensus was in no small part the work of Bill Buckley and the reformed Communists who founded *National Review*.

It is probably no exaggeration to say that hostility to the Red Menace has been the primary impulse behind post–World War II American conservatism. Rightly or wrongly, the traditional conservative values of moderation and restraint have come to be regarded as inadequate to deal with the threat from Moscow and Peking. And antistatism itself has stopped at the water's edge. As a result, civil libertarians like Peter Vierick and schematic anarchists like Murray Rothbard have been read out of the conservative movement. Initially, however, realignment of the Right was not a function of disagreement about strategy toward the Soviet Union so much as conflict over the zealotry of a single anti-Communist crusader—Senator Joseph McCarthy.

Tail Gunner Bill

In February 1977, NBC devoted an entire evening to a docudrama entitled "Tail Gunner Joe." Purporting to be an objective treatment of the McCarthy Era, this video polemic featured Peter Boyle in such a crude caricature of the Wisconsin demagogue as to make Boyle's performance in *Young Frankenstein* seem subtly modulated by comparison. This travesty and Buckley's response to it (to defend McCarthy by attacking his enemies) suggest that the debate over McCarthyism is still very much with us.

That debate has been characterized all too often by an attempt on the part of McCarthy's adversaries and defenders alike to mythologize the man and what he stood for. Only when we get beyond the mythology do we begin to realize that McCarthy and the recent American Left may have been largely responsible for each other. I suspect that the blunders of the left made McCarthy an historical inevitability, while the senator's own more histrionic blunders did more to enhance than to destroy the respectability of his opponents.

In *McCarthy and His Enemies* (1954), Buckley and Brent Bozell make the case that Soviet infiltration of the American government in the late 1940s and early 1950s threatened to shift the balance of international power. The Alger Hiss case proved both the existence of such infiltration and the unwillingness of certain government officials to take it seriously. As a result, this situation inspired a Manichaean populist backlash which failed to make sufficient distinctions between judgmental errors and intentional subversion.

In the course of his later criticisms of Robert Welch and the John Birch Society, Buckley maintains that strategic setbacks for the West do not necessarily prove treason within the American government. And yet, he seems unwilling to acknowledge that McCarthy was habitually guilty of making just such an inference. Although Buckley and Bozell are

careful to distinguish between security and loyalty risks, they are frequently forced to concede that McCarthy rarely did so. Beause of the
senator's rhetorical carelessness, liberals who unwittingly belonged to
Communist-infiltrated organizations were often branded as disloyal
Americans.

It is ideologically tenable for conservatives to argue that American
security is not well served when a preponderance of foreign policy
decisions are made by persons of leftist sympathies; however, it is quite
another thing to say—as Buckley and Bozell did in 1954—that "as long
as McCarthyism fixes its goal with its present precision, it is a movement
around which men of good will and stern morality can close ranks."[2] In
point of fact, the men of good will and stern morality who constituted
the United States Senate (some of whom were conservative Republicans)
finally closed ranks to censure the *imprecision* of McCarthyism. It was
these men (not Communists or fellow travelers) who ultimately proved
to be McCarthy's undoing.

One who relied solely on the Buckley-Bozell study for an understanding of the McCarthy controversy would think that only liberal dupes
opposed the scatter-shot tactics of Tail Gunner Joe. And yet, such a
staunch anti-Communist as Whittaker Chambers admitted to living "in
terror that Senator McCarthy will one day make some irreparable blun-
der which will play directly into the hands of our common enemy and
discredit the whole anti-Communist effort for a long while to come."[3]
Indeed, Peter Vierick summed up the opinion of many conservatives
when he argued that the Communist cause was served by both Owen
Lattimore and Joseph McCarthy: Lattimore "by the way he defended it,"
and McCarthy "by the way he attacked it".[4]

One of Buckley's basic strategies in defending McCarthy has always
been to castigate the "hysteria" of McCarthy's opponents. It is a device
which may work well enough on the debate platform, but one which also
violates the fundamental rules of logic. One cannot justify McCarthy
simply by pointing a finger at his critics. It is perhaps closer to the truth
to say that the man was both reprehensible himself and the cause of
reprehensibility in others. The most that we can infer from the intem-
perance of McCarthy's critics is that the relative impunity with which the
senator was attacked tended to belie the notion that he had effectively
silenced free speech in America.

If Buckley's defense of the Wisconsin Torquemada is too deadly
serious even to be regarded as amusing camp, his frequently arch
denunciation of domestic Stalinists is something else again. Indeed, his

January 1977 hatchet job on the egregious Lillian Hellman (*H*, 139–52) is the sort of fare around which men of good will and stern morality will always close ranks.

Like Henry Fielding, Buckley realizes that the most crippling form of personal abuse is ridicule. Consequently, he paints Saint Lillian as an over-rated hack whose political posturings reek of disingenuousness. Is she, as a fawning Garry Wills maintains, "the greatest woman playwright in American history"? Probably. But isn't saying so "on the order of celebrating the tallest building in Wichita, Kansas?" (*H*, 140). And what hideous martyrdom did "the greatest woman playwright" suffer for her convictions? "She had to sell her country house! She had to fire her cook and gardener! She had to give up a million-dollar contract! She had to take a part-time job in a department store! Her lover [Dashiell Hammett] had to go to jail!" (*H*, 141). Buckley deflates these very real—if overdramatized—deprivations with his bouquet of exclamation points and with a dead-pan reference to Thomas More.

A bit later in the essay, we learn that Miss Hellman's paramour Dashiell Hammett was on the board of the Civil Rights Congress "which voted to refuse its support of the cause of James Kutcher, a paraplegic veteran who had been discharged as a government clerk because he belonged to the Trotskyite Socialist Workers Party." Of course, according to the Moscow party line, the only right owed to a Trotskyist is that of an ice pick in the back of the head. As that knee-jerk Stalinist Paul Robeson observed about this controversy: "you don't ask Jews to help a Nazi or Negroes to help the KKK."[5] Quite appropriately, in October 1976, Lillian Hellman won the Paul Robeson Award from Actor's Equity in recognition of her "'concern for and service to fellow humans'" (*H*, 149).

The Protracted Conflict

If, as Buckley maintains, the struggle between Communist despotism and Western democracy is a grand morality play, then symbolic gestures take on a kind of sacramental importance. Neither President Eisenhower's inviting Khrushchev to visit the United States in 1959 nor President Ford's not inviting Solzhenitsyn to visit the White House in 1975 materially strengthened Soviet tyranny by so much as a single strand of barbed wire; however, by showing greater civility to the slavemasters of the Gulag Archipelago than to their victims, America partially undercuts its claim to being a moral as well as a military power.

Speaking before an audience in Carnegie Hall in 1959, Buckley warned of the grave implications of welcoming Khrushchev to our shores. The damage, he argued, was not in what the Soviet premier could do to the United States, but in what the United States in inviting him already had done to itself. The argument is made in eloquent and impassioned tones:

That [Khrushchev] should achieve orthodox diplomatic recognition not three years after shocking history itself by the brutalities of Budapest; months after endorsing the shooting down of an unarmed American plane; only weeks since he last shrieked his intention in *Foreign Affairs,* of demolishing the West should it show any resistance to the march of socialism; only days since publishing in an American magazine his undiluted resolve to enslave the citizens of Free Berlin—that such an introduction should end up constituting his credentials for a visit to America will teach him something about the West some of us wish he might never have known.[6]

What it is about the West that Buckley says he would rather Khrushchev didn't know is that we are a pragmatic rather than an idealistic people. Even if the Soviets are consummate opportunists who believe that the end justifies *any* means, they at least have ends to which they are committed. The West, on the other hand, seems to have lost the will to prevail. One wonders whether the will to endure can be far behind.

When Solzhenitsyn emerged like an Old Testament prophet from the depths of a modern Gehenna, his jeremiad on Western decadence did not sit well with the Yankee Doodle Dandy crowd. But they could hardly say: if he doesn't like it here, why doesn't he go back to Russia? So, the only feasible alternative was to ignore him. When Gerry Ford, on the advice of the image-conscious Henry Kissinger, proved too busy to invite the Russian author to tea at the White House, not a few men of good will and stern morality began to wonder if detente were not really the moral equivalent of emasculation.

To put the Solzhenitsyn episode in perspective, we need only ask ourselves when was the last time that a Communist leader failed to meet with an American dissident for fear of offending the United States government. Indeed, Buckley recalls that when he was in the Soviet Union in connection with a United States Information Agency Exhibit opened to "foster international understanding," the Soviet press devoted two sentences to that exhibit, while concentrating much of the rest of its coverage on Angela Davis, "who was touring the Soviet Union to denounce the United States" (*H,* 51). Lamenting the demonic integrity of the Communist vision, Buckley observes: "How clearly, every day that we log the activities of the free nations of the world in juxtaposition with those of the enemy, their moral—yes, *moral*—superiority strikes us" (*H,* 50).

Buckley's view of the Soviet Union, however, is not based solely on ideological predisposition. The man who would have barred Khrushchev from our shores in 1959 had mellowed enough by 1970 to make his own trek to the Finland Station. As part of the USIA tour which lost top billing to Angela Davis, Bourgeois Bill came face to face with the red serfs and their Bolshevik overlords—an experience which he recounts in "A Million and One Nights in Soviet Russia" (*I,* 105–32).

Although much of this essay is given over to Buckley's wry observations about American and Soviet bureaucracy and to grumblings about the surliness and incompetence of the Russian serving class, some genuine moral insights do emerge. One recalls, for example, Buckley's cajoling his tour guide into allowing him to visit the czar's Winter Palace. There, he strolls in the garden where a doomed Nicholas once rode his bicycle around the few pathways left open to him by his Bolshevik guards. Those guards would entertain themselves by poking sticks into the wheels of the czar's bicycle, "causing him to catapult over onto the ground, whence he would lift himself, silently, deliberately, unreproachfully, remount the bicycle, unminding of the taunters, who for half such an aggression would thirty days earlier have been knouted and hanged; and head back toward his family, so as not to interrupt, by any melodramatic defiance, the grisly end that awaited them all, sixteen months later, in the cellar at Ekaterinburg" (*I,* 129). This depiction of the nobility of the czar and the gratuitous cruelty of his captors is calculated to stir pity and indignation in the Tory breast like nothing since Edmund Burke's teary tribute to a condemned Marie Antoinette.

On the surface, it would seem to make good ideological sense for the Communists simply to raze the czar's palace. "[B]ut of course they have always shown that certain caution that many iconoclasts show":

Thus, at Leningrad, they convert the cathedral of Kazan, where the czars prayed, into an "Institute of Religion and Atheism"; but they do not tear it down, whether for reasons of husbandry, or because they believe that the profanation of a cathedral is high-class revolutionary piquancy. . . . [Or perhaps] there is a third reason, which is that the Russians, even the Communist

Russians, cannot practice wholehearted Orwellianism; *i.e.*, they cannot induce themselves to *destroy* that which they disapprove of (unless it is a human being). They sublimate it (as with the Kazan Cathedral); or ignore it (as with Tsarskoe Selo); or profiteer from it (as with the crown jewels one pays to see). But they do not *destroy* it, for some reason; a reason the understanding of which would leave us better understanding the Soviet Union, and hence the world (*I*, 129).

Significantly, Buckley refrains from drawing sweeping conclusions from his "million and one nights" in the worker's paradise. Nor does he prescribe an appropriate Western response to what he has seen. Instead, a kind of stoic pessimism pervades the conclusion of his essay. When his tour guide asks that he send her some books when he returns to America, he promises to send her what she wants: *Peyton Place, Hotel, Valley of the Dolls*, and *The Carpetbaggers*. There is no point, he surmises, in sending her *The Cancer Ward*. For "*Nina does not want to be troubled;* and I would not want to trouble her, not unless the prospects for success were assured, or at least reasonably assured" (*I*, 131–32). "We waited for years for the American Army," a Polish intellectual later tells Buckley "— commenting on the recent visit of our astronauts. 'And when it came, there were just three of them'" (*I*, 132).

The China Syndrome

If anti-Communism has been the chief passion of the post–World War II American Right, that fact is not solely attributable to the prodigious infamies of Uncle Joe Stalin. Of at least equal importance was the ascendency of Maoism in mainland China. Not only was China more populous than Russia, and—hence—a greater potential danger, but its fall was viewed as an American defeat in a way that the fall of the Romanoff empire never was. After all, Chiang Kai-shek was not just an American ally; he was a veritable embodiment of Western theocracy—a sort of Asian Franco. Such a man could lose only if God had withdrawn his blessing from the American cause. Or if the Devil had infiltrated the American State Department. (To a large extent, the career of Joe McCarthy was predicated on the necessity of proving the latter in order to disprove the former.)

As hard-headed as they are on matters of profit and loss, conservatives can be downright sentimental about such things as governments-in-exile. We may never know when the precise moment was that Bill Buckley stopped believing that the Taiwanese would retake the Chinese mainland, but it is almost certain that for him that moment represented more a loss of faith in America's resolve than in Chiang's. Indeed, as he suggests in an address delivered to the National Defense Research Institute of Taiwan, our dealings with China serve as a kind of touchstone of the American spirit. "The vivid contrast," he declares, "is between, on the one hand, the hopes and plans of the leadership of your movement and, on the other, the worries and fears of the leadership of the Liberal movement in America. We are more powerful than you by far; richer than you by many billions of dollars. But by your example, we may yet live" (*R,* 44).

It is surely one of the supreme ironies of recent history that our renunciation of Taiwan's claim to sovereignty over the mainland was effected not by the accommodation of an American Chamberlain, but by the *realpolitik* of an American Bismarck. When Richard Nixon announced his decision to break bread with Mao, James and William Buckley heard the news in the living room of the California governor's mansion, where they were breaking bread with Ronald Reagan. The *zeitgeist* had progressed so far that evening that, of those three diners, only Bill Buckley suspended his formal support of the Nixon administration. And that fit of moral pique lasted only long enough for right-wing insurgent John Ashbrook to lose the 1972 New Hampshire primary to *both* Nixon and peace candidate Pete McCloskey (the latter of whom polled twice as many votes as Ashbrook). Indeed, by the time the press plane accompanying Air Force One to China pulled out of Washington, Buckley was on board.

Although Buckley was *with* the China party, he was never *of* it in the sense of being an enthusiastic participant in the trip. Rather, he was like the censor who watches pornographic movies, not because he enjoys them, but because it is his civic duty to warn more impressionable mortals of the danger such movies pose. The effect of what he describes, however, is similar to that which Judge Woolsey attributed to *Ulysses:* "somewhat emetic, [but] nowhere . . . an aphrodisiac."[7] Nevertheless, it is great fun for inveterate Nixon haters who don't mind whether they get their thrills from the left or the right.

While observing the effusive toasts offered by the leader of the free world to the war lords of what was once an "outlaw" nation, Buckley finds the spectacle no less ludicrous than if "Sir Hartley Shawcross had suddenly risen from the prosecutor's stand at Nuremberg and descended to embrace Goering and Goebbels and Doenitz and Hess, begging them to join with him in the making of a better world." That anyone would imagine a moral difference between these two scenes reminds us only "that history is indeed the polemics of the victor" (*I*, 87).

If it did nothing else, Nixon's "long march" to China dramatically confirmed America's philosophical acceptance of coexistence. In so doing, it sounded the death knell for what Buckley calls the "Wilsonian idea"—the notion that the West bears a solemn obligation to make the world safe for democracy. Perhaps the nuclear age itself has made such retrenchment inevitable; however, it is a development which militant advocates of democracy cannot help but find disquieting. Despite profound differences over specific matters of policy, conservative anti-Communists and Wilsonian liberals had long shared the assumption that nations ought to be held to some standard of civilized behavior. Although the coming of detente did not necessarily make might into right, it went a long way toward exempting those with nuclear might from the obligation to do right as a condition for earning international deference.

Unfortunately, the alternative to such Machiavellian cynicism is the hardline anti-Communist notion that the world would be better dead than red.[8] This notion, it seems to me, falls prey to the fallacy of universalization. What it fails to consider is the qualitative difference between urging martyrdom for individuals and acquiescing to the effective martyrdom of the human race. Since an individual's world must always end for him at the moment of death, the argument goes, there is no essential difference between falling on a conventional field of battle and being incinerated in a nuclear holocaust.

The problem with this analysis, however, is its reliance on a concept of valor which modern warfare has rendered obsolete. Historically, soldiers have been willing to face death because they believed that in so doing they would help to preserve a decent life for those who were left behind—family, friends, countrymen. In contrast, nuclear war does not involve sacrifice for a greater good, but conceivably the obliteration of all mankind and, hence, of all human values. To fail to appreciate this salient distinction is finally to equate the heroism of a Winston Churchill with the madness of a Jim Jones.

One need not view those of the Buckley persuasion as wild-eyed bombers intent on nuking the cosmos to see the danger of applying traditional just-war theories to what might well be an apocalyptic confrontation. As Buckley himself realizes, those who extend the "better dead than red" position to the entire globe must answer the argument that "although some things may be worth dying for, it cannot be worth dying for nothing, which is what would be left over in the event of a nuclear exchange."[9] Because Buckley regards life under Communism as a fate worse than death, he has no difficulty in answering that argument. Other men of good will and stern morality, however, might think it better for the planet to live to fight another day than to go down in flames; to place its hope for *temporal* salvation in an insurrection of the enslaved rather than in a resurrection of the dead. Indeed, to believe otherwise is to envision the day when it may be necessary to destroy the world in order to save it.

Chapter Four
Dubious Battles

The nuclear capacity of the superpowers has created something of a stalemate in East-West relations. Although the eagle and the bear have cast many dirty looks at each other, outright conflict has been sublimated into proxy skirmishes between client states. Indeed, from the late fifties to the mid-sixties, the principal obsession of American foreign policy was not Russia but Cuba. Then, from the mid-sixties to the early seventies, it was Vietnam that occupied center stage.

As the Cold War continued to manifest itself in strange ways and exotic locations, a number of thoughtful foreign policy observers began to suggest that the developed nations—be they Communist or capitalist—had less to fear from each other than from the emerging nations of the Third World. The most important conflicts, according to this view, were not between East and West, but between North and South. (Since the survivors of a nuclear war—assuming that there would be any—would be disproportionately nonwhite,[1] such a war would mark the end of international supremacy for *both* the United States and the Soviet Union.) Hence, it might be instructive for us to examine William Buckley's comments on America's dealings with the inchoate superpowers—the Clark Kent nations of the world.

Cuba Libre

When Dr. Fidel Castro (as he was known in liberal circles) rode down from the mountains of Cuba to deliver that *scepter'd isle* from the Mafia to the Kremlin, American conservatives experienced an uneasy sense of *déjà vu*. Before Mao had taken over China, we were assured by the Owen Lattimores of this world that what we were witnessing was nothing more than agrarian reform. Now, a decade later, a new crop of savants was telling us that Dr. Castro was the George Washington of Cuba. It wasn't long, however, before *Señor* Washington started sounding like Lenin and acting like Robespierre.

The acquisition of Cuba represented a major advance in Soviet imperialism. As long as the commissars confined their barbarities to Eastern Europe, they could claim a kind of manifest destiny (not unlike Abraham Lincoln's Illinois farmer who wasn't greedy for land, wanting only what joined his). Cuba, however, was Russia's first noncontiguous satellite. Moreover, it was the land that Teddy Roosevelt had liberated from European dominance. If the Monroe Doctrine and good old Yankee Doodle chauvinism meant anything, America could not tolerate an enemy outpost ninety miles from Key West.

The fiasco of the Bay of Pigs in 1961 and the standoff of the missile crisis in 1962 placed the United States on the defensive in its campaign against Castro, and not even the combined forces of the CIA and the American underworld could return Cuba to the *status quo ante*. With military measures thus neutralized, ideologues of the right were reduced to bickering over "who lost Cuba." This, Buckley does in "Herbert Matthews and Fidel Castro: I got my job through *The New York Times*" (*R*, 46–53).

Citing relevant passages from Matthews's dispatches on Cuba, Buckley demonstrates the uncritical infatuation which the *New York Times'* foreign correspondent felt for Castro's revolution. Indeed, Matthews's prestige was such that the State Department gave more credence to his views than to those of America's own ambassador. Thus, "it could be said—with a little license—that Matthews was to Castro what Owen Lattimore was to Red China, and that *The New York Times* was Matthews' Institute of Pacific Relations" (*R*, 46).

Had Buckley been using the vocabulary which his friend James Burnham later developed and which Jeanne Kirkpatrick has done so much to popularize, he would have accused Matthews of straining at an authoritarian gnat to the point of swallowing a totalitarian camel. From a strategic—and probably even a human rights—standpoint, it is better to go with a pro-American goon like Batista or the Shah of Iran than usher in the likes of Castro or the Ayatollah Khomeini. Unfortunately, doctrinaire antifascists like Matthews assume that anyone intent on overthrowing an evil right-wing regime must, by definition, be a friend of liberal democracy. Buckley feels that American foreign policy has shown undue deference toward such views. Speaking of the Kennedy White House, he writes, "the new U.S. Administration must answer the question why, the more offensive Fidel Castro seemed to this country, the madder we got at General Trujillo" (*R, 53*).

The issue which Buckley raises here really extends beyond the question of one's preference for a Batista in the hand or a Castro in the bush. He is at least implicitly asking to what extent human rights considerations should ouweigh American strategic interests in determining our support for a given regime. This issue, however, is not one which divides simply along liberal and conservative lines. If there is hypocrisy on the left when it comes to dealing with human rights, what are we to say of supposedly pragmatic right wingers who wish to scrap the *realpolitik* of detente for the Wilsonian idealism of linkage? I suspect that the only way that a functioning government can take a totally consistent stand toward human rights in other countries is to ignore them altogether.[2]

It should be obvious that no nation can long exist without at some time having to do business with unsavory regimes. Senator Fulbright tried to resolve this difficulty by arguing that "Insofar as a nation is content to practice its doctrines within its own frontiers, that nation, however repugnant its ideology, is one with which we have no proper quarrel" (*EE, 34*). Such a policy, consistently pursued, would allow us to deal with Batista, but would also prevent us from reacting to the suppression of dissidents within the Soviet Union. Because Henry Kissinger attempted to follow this amoralistic *via media,* he was roundly castigated from both ends of the political spectrum. What his ideological critics failed to realize, however, is that negotiating with an individual terrorist for the release of a handful of hostages is appeasement; while negotiating with a terrorist nation for the release of a hostage world is statesmanship.

The Way We Played the Game

Speaking of that sublimated form of war known as sports, Grantland Rice sagely observed: "When the great scorer up above / Goes to mark against your name / It matters not whether you won or lost / It's how you played the game." According to any objective measurement, America played the game very badly in Vietnam. (The late Allard Lowenstein once remarked that he could understand the position that we should win and get out, but not the actual policy that we should lose and stay in. Whatever else Vietnam may have taught us, it demonstrated the limitations of limited war.) Since everyone old enough to have watched the evening news during the Vietnam era already knows the official positions of the various administrations that fought the war as well as the sundry leftist critiques of those positions, the only point of view not suffering from overexposure is the independent conservative one represented by William Buckley.

Despite the many serious essays he has written on the subject, Buckley's most discussed contribution to the Vietnam debate was in the form of a hoax. In 1971, after the *New York Times* had made a big splash by publishing the Pentagon Papers, Buckley and several editors and experts fabricated their own set of documents and passed them off in *National Review* as authentic. After five days, Buckley called a press conference in order to disclose that the papers were fabrications and to give his reasons for the venture. This prank cost Buckley considerable credibility—especially among fellow conservatives who, in the tradition of Queen Victoria, were not amused.

In a way, the Buckley papers incident is characteristic of its perpetrator's stance toward Vietnam—he believed the cause so inherently noble as to sanction more aggressive and devious policies than were then being pursued. It made little sense, he surmised, to fight according to the Marquis of Queensbury rules when one's opponent was allowed to kick and gouge.

From a purely strategic standpoint, many of Buckley's insights seem plausible. For one thing, he argued in December 1969 that our military resources were being squandered in an attempt "to track down and eliminate supplies which entered into the country in the first place via a couple of bottlenecks visible to every seagull on the coastline of North Vietnam and Cambodia."[3] He further argued that blocking those accesses "would be the humane thing to do. . . . [It] would save not only American lives, not only South Vietnamese lives, but also North Vietnamese lives" (*GL,* 269). However, military and humanitarian considerations took a back seat to political ones. We simply could not give the appearance of violating the "neutrality" of Laos and Cambodia, even though our enemy had long treated the borders of those countries as a geographical fiction.

In April 1970, Richard Nixon took the politically inexpedient action of sending American troops into Cambodia. Predictably, this move was applauded by Buckley and other advocates of a more assertive American strategy. And, just as predictably, it created a storm of protest throughout the nation—particularly on college campuses. To Buckley's mind, such protest amounted to hysteria.

Considerably less hysterical, though equally wrong-headed, was the criticism which greeted South Vietnamese operations in Laos a year later. Buckley cites these operations as evidence of the success of Nixon's policy of Vietnamization. He reasons that one of the benefits of transferring military responsibility for the war to the South Vietnamese was that a measure of the political responsibility for making hard decisions was transferred as well. "[W]e slip quietly out of the headlines," he writes, "for the simple reason that foreign troops drawn osmotically into Laos in defense of their own country make a very small headline if they are South Vietnamese, and a very large headline only if they are American, or if they are being directed by Americans" (*I*, 143).

If we move from strategic to moral considerations, however, Buckley's position on Vietnam becomes much less convincing. Consider, for example, his reflections on the My Lai massacre. This American atrocity could not be excused as an unavoidable by-product of war (as when a pilot bombing a military target at 30,000 feet also wipes out a village of civilians). Hence, the antiwar crowd pointed smugly to My Lai as an example of the extent to which Vietnam had brutalized the sensibilities of American soldiers. It was not enough for supporters of the war to declare the cold-blooded murder of women and children an aberration; they also had to account for the fact that the good guys could be guilty of the kind of action we so roundly condemned at Nuremberg. Buckley attempts to do precisely that in what is for him an uncharacteristically fatuous essay.

One of the more appealing aspects of conservative thought is its insistence on free will and moral responsibility. And yet, what Buckley says about My Lai sounds very much like the sort of drivel one hears from liberal apologists for domestic criminals. He contends that Calley and cohorts were "unbalanced by a society . . . deprived of the strength of religious sanctions, a society hugely devoted to hedonism, to permissive egalitarianism, to irresponsibility, to an indifference to authority and the law" (*GL*, 254). He even goes so far as to cite Berkeley as a better metonymic explanation for the massacres than Vietnam.

If the liberal response to Cambodia could be characterized as hysterical, then Buckley's explanation for My Lai hardly qualifies as grace under pressure. Assuming that there is a domestic analogue to the My Lai personality, it can be found more easily in the psychopathology of the Hell's Angels than in the panty-raid mentality of the Free Speech Movement. The massacre, as practiced by white man and Indian alike, was an accepted part of our frontier tradition. Vietnam, then, was simply a new frontier.

It is possible to blame My Lai on the war itself without necessarily impugning the motives for American involvement. In a guerilla conflict which involves civilian combatants, women and children are no longer just women and children, but potential grenade tossers. The Viet Cong acknowledged as much by liquidating at least 2,750 civilians at Hué. The difference between this action and the one at My Lai (other than the fact that the V.C. killed about 100 times as many civilians as Calley) is that Hué was part of official Communist strategy, whereas My Lai was an offense which resulted in a court-martial.

That American tactics in Vietnam were nasty enough to be reprehensible (the napalming of babies and the like) but not nasty enough to be successful tells us something about the nature of modern warfare. Technology has progressed to the point where it is now almost impossible to wage a prolonged war without incurring a large number of civilian casualties. (Since Vietnam was both a technological and a guerilla conflict, the incidence of civilian deaths was particularly high.) Under such circumstances, a modern war effort can be either successful or morally scrupulous, but not both (America's in Vietnam was neither). The situation is further complicated by the fact that people like Hitler, Stalin, and Ho Chi Minh do not consult the same moral theologians as do the Western democracies.

For the pacifist, the only acceptable stance is to opt out of modern warfare altogether. To do so, however, is to risk creating the sort of world which Yeats envisioned in "The Second Coming"—where "The best lack all conviction, while the worst / Are full of passionate intensity." Consequently, most persons would vote for taking arms in an unavoidable conflict with Attila the Hun. Still, it is possible for men of good will and stern morality to question whether such a dubious battle as Vietnam was necessary to keep the Hun at bay.

Blackford Comes to Dumbarton

In 1973, while the nation was wallowing in Watergate, Richard Nixon made an overture to the American right by appointing William Buckley as a delegate to the twenty-eighth General Assembly of the United Nations. Considering the fact that Buckley was then one of Nixon's harshest critics, *Chicago Sun-Times'* columnist Irv Kupcinet

wondered whether "the President [was] adopting a 'kill 'em with kindness' philosophy" toward his opponents.' [4] After reading Buckley's account of his service in the United Nations, one suspects that Nixon's
intention was to kill not with kindness but with boredom. To subject a
man with Buckley's reverence for language to the prolix dissimulations
of U.N. oratory is not unlike assigning a concert master the task of
teaching piano to tone-deaf children.

That Buckley took the assignment at all was, by his own confession,
an exercise in "pure, undiluted Walter Mittyism" (UN, 13). He had
been appointed by U.N. Ambassador John Scali to the Committee on
Human Rights, a forum from which he imagined himself holding the
U.N.—and the world—spellbound with readings from Solzhenitsyn
and with graphic descriptions of Communist brutality. After all, the
position to which he was appointed had previously been held by Eleanor
Roosevelt and Daniel Patrick Moynihan, neither of whom were known as
shrinking violets.

Walter Mitty, of course, performed heroics only in his dreams. And so
it would be for Buckley. The law governing U.S. participation in the
United Nations makes all delegates creatures of the president. (Buckley
surmises that this was the only way Harry Truman had of keeping Mrs.
Roosevelt on any kind of leash.) Unfortunately, the policy which
Buckley's president was expounding was the decidely un-Mittyesque
detente. When the constricted nature of his role became apparent,
Buckley considered resigning but held back from doing so rather than
expose the fact that he had initially misunderstood the nature of the job
he had accepted. In order to prevent the experience from being a total
waste of time, however, he resolved to keep a journal which would be
published after his term was over.

The chief impression which one derives from Buckley's account is of
the strident hypocrisy and self-importance of Third World and Communist delegates. That and the sheer tedium of having to listen to them.
For Buckley, the ultimate U.N. figure was the late Saudi Arabian
Ambassador Jamil Baroody. Indeed, the author argues that "the popular
image of the United Nations as the densest collection of oratorical bores
in the history of the world is owing as much to Baroody as to the next one
hundred senior delegates who have served there" (UN, 69). Not only has
he been at the U.N. since its founding, but he talks ten times as much as
his nearest competitor. And he never tires of repeating himself. To be
sure, "there is very little option for someone who speaks so much. If he

had mastered the entire sum of human knowledge, he would still need, perforce, to repeat himself after a week or two" (*UN,* 69).

Reminding us that Mr. Baroody is the representative of King Faisal, Buckley quotes the Saudi moralist's denunciation of "those who exercise excessive power or acquire superfluous wealth [and] are too preoccupied with their own achievements and so dazzled by the adulation of the masses that they fail to pay sufficient attention to the fundamental human rights of others." He also spoke of the "'unstable hunger for excessive wealth' a fortnight after Saudi Arabia had tripled the price of its oil" (*UN,* 242).

If Baroody was the most enduring presence at the U.N., he was not necessarily the most outrageous. On one occasion, when the Chilean ambassador was defaming the good name of Dr. Castro, Cuban Foreign Minister Raul Roa rushed the podium, followed by four Cuban body-guards. "Roa was screaming *'hijo de puta!'* (son of a whore), and *'maricon'* (fag)—two all-purpose but very high-velocity Spanish swear words. At this point miscellaneous Latin Americans rose to block Roa's way—and Roa's bodyguards were seen poised to raise their pistols. It is the judgment of those closest by that shooting was very narrowly avoided" (*UN,* 118–19). Thus is business transacted in the world's last best hope for peace.

Then, there was the time that Field Marshall Idi Amin, president of Uganda, pretender to the throne of Scotland, and—in the words of Richard Nixon—"goddamn cannibal asshole" decided to address the General Assembly. Once voted by U.S. Foreign Service officials as the world's single most incompetent leader, Amin was the sort of figure who might have emerged from a collaboration of Evelyn Waugh and the Marquis de Sade. (Ever the ecologist, he never killed an opponent he wasn't willing to eat.) When Amin resolved to share his inestimable wisdom with other peace-loving types, he cabled Golda Meir to request that his audience include several leaders of the Israeli army (Generals Dayan, Rabin, et al.). Unfortunately, those men were then preoccupied with fighting the Yom Kippur War. Therefore, "it is perhaps under-standable that there is no recorded response to General Amin's cable" (*UN,* 147).

It is perhaps just as well that the Israeli brass ignored Amin's invita-tion, since his discourse was to be on the Protocols of the Learned Elders of Zion, a document which had just come to the field marshall's attention although it had been demonstrated to be a forgery some time before his birth. With the current Elders of Zion indisposed to hear his address, Amin canceled his trip to New York in favor of making a U.N. Day speech in Uganda. (The American ambassador considered walking out on that speech, but decided against doing so: since such a gesture was not a Ugandan tradition, those in attendance would have interpreted it as having been prompted by a "call of nature" [*UN*, 149].) The substance of the General's remarks was that at 9:00 A.M. that day (0600 Greenwich Mean Time) God had informed His servant Idi Amin of the desirability of a cease-fire in the Middle East. The fourth estate, however, had scooped the Almighty by having informed the rest of the world of the cease-fire which had been consummated the previous day.

Bereft of personal Mittyesque aspirations, Buckley concludes his U.N. memoir with a fantasy scenario in which the General Assembly is taken from within by a faction intent on purging all vestiges of hypocrisy from that august body. No more would the world be subjected to Soviet pontifications on disarmament or Chinese homilies on human rights. Nor would the Arabs *"be permitted to speak about the plight of the Less Developed Countries without foreswearing the cartelization of their oil;* [or] *the Africans . . .* [to] *talk about racism until after subduing the leaders of Uganda, the Central African Republic, and Burundi, for a starter"* (UN, 253–54). And the delegates from Eastern Europe would be required to *"wear red uniforms when they appear on the floor and, before rising to speak, . . . seek explicit and public permission from the delegate of the Soviet Union"* (UN, 254). Short of making such reforms, the United Nations is likely to remain what Delegate Buckley found it to be—"the most concentrated assault on moral reality in the history of free institutions" (*UN*, 257).

A Man A Plan A Canal Panama

During the 1980 presidential campaign, conservative Republicans entertained themselves with a story of Theodore Roosevelt's return from the grave. Needless to say, the world which our most chauvinistic president found was vastly different from the one which he had known. Defeat in Vietnam followed by detente and a public backlash against militarism were hard enough for the hero of San Juan Hill to fathom, but the humiliating spectacle of the Iranian hostage crisis was quite simply beyond his comprehension. "The next thing you're going to be telling me," sighed an exasperated T.R., "is that we gave back the Panama Canal."

Even a few years later, it is difficult to remember the passions evoked by Senate consideration of the Panama Canal treaties in the spring of 1978. Although the treaties had been negotiated during the administrations of four American presidents (two Democrats and two Republicans), the mail-order savants of the New Right ascribed responsibility for the final product to the hapless Jimmy Carter. Indeed, the issue was so fraught with jingoistic symbolism that the eventual ratification of the treaties ranks as a minor political and diplomatic miracle. No small part of the credit for that miracle is owing to the strange coalition of bipartisan and trans-ideological support which the treaties received from opinion makers outside the Senate. To the chagrin of what George Will calls the "pip-squeak Right," Bill Buckley was part of that coalition.

On Super Bowl Sunday 1978, sports fans awaiting that year's championship clash between the Dallas Cowboys and the Denver Broncos were afforded some pregame diversion by a special segment of *Firing Line*—a super oratorical clash between Buckley and Ronald Reagan on the topic of the Canal treaties. Not only was the topic of interest to the nation, but the anomaly of America's two most prominent conservatives' opposing each other on a matter of public policy was a spectacle in its own right. Indeed, Buckley himself expressed amazement that Governor Reagan "should make a mistake." "But of course it happens to everyone," he conceded. "I fully expect that some day *I'll* be wrong about something" (*H*, 229).

After reaffirming his long-standing contempt for doctrinaire anticolonialism, Buckley contends that the treaties in question would serve the military, economic, and spiritual self-interest of the United States. Following the example of William Howard Taft, treaty proponents argue that the United States should not want to own anything in Panama, only to have access to the canal that runs through Panama. Such access would be guaranteed by the treaties and, in times of military conflict, would be more likely to be vouchsafed if we could count on the good will and "cooperation of the 2 million people in whose territory the Canal lies, [and] whose personnel already do three-quarters of the work required to keep the Canal open" (*H*, 232). (If the conflict is nuclear, the Canal would—of course—"revert to a land-mass, and the first survivor who makes his way across the Isthmus will relive a historical experience, 'like stout Cortez when with eagle eyes he stared at the Pacific—and all his men looked at each other with a wild surmise—silent, upon a peak in Darien'" [*H*, 231].[5])

The economic argument for the treaties rests on the fact that America would retain revenue from the use of the Canal while being relieved of certain expenses which derive from outright ownership. Although treaty opponents assert that the totality of U.S. dealings with Panama would put Uncle Sam at a $60 million a year disadvantage, they neglect to note that this money would come from income generated by the Canal rather than from the pockets of American taxpayers. Besides, we pay the Turks *billions* of dollars a year for the right to defend them from the Soviet Union without receiving any off-setting revenue—not even a royalty on the Turkish heroin sold on the streets of America.

Given the military advantages of the treaties and what are, at worst, negligible economic consequences, little purpose would be served by retaining titular ownership of the Canal. Under these circumstances, it would be a vulgar and unnecessary display of U.S. machismo not to ratify the treaties. Better not to spill our seed in a backwater like Panama when it might be needed for facing down the Soviets on more important diplomatic fronts.

Alas, not everyone was persuaded by Buckley's subtle dialectic. For example, Mrs. Albert G. Frisk of Weston, Connecticut took thirty minutes to inform an *NR* staff member of her displeasure with the magazine's editor. Not only did she disagree with his Panama stand, but "couldn't discern a single reason for it in . . . [his] debate with that nice Mr. Reagan." Mrs. Frisk, incidentally, was named for Martha Washington and had a great-great-grandfather at Ripon. About which the object of her wrath remarked: "Wasn't Ripon where we gave away slavery?"[6]

Chapter Five
A Wealth of Notions

Conservatives probably figure that America got off the track about the time that Jefferson transformed the common-law litany "life, liberty, and property" into "life, liberty, and the pursuit of happiness." Indeed, welfare-state liberalism might well be defined as the pursuit of happiness at the expense of property. For economic libertarians, such a trade-off is doubly distressing. First, they regard any happiness thus pursued as illusory. And second, they consider the limitation of property rights to be an atrocity in comparison to which the suppression of mere political freedom pales into insignificance. Mankind's last free lunch, after all, was in the Garden of Eden.

Minding the Store

In *Up From Liberalism,* William Buckley describes an ideological watershed which occurred midway through Franklin Roosevelt's second term. At that time, Roosevelt's advisors were groping for a way to assuage public concern over the mushrooming national debt. They found the solution to their problem in a sophistical insight gleaned from the *carpe-diem* economics of John Maynard Keynes. The "intoxicating political effect" of their discovery is depicted in a cartoon which appeared in the *Washington Times Herald:* "In the center [of the cartoon], seated on a throne, was a jubilant FDR, cigarette tilted almost vertically, grinning from ear to ear. Dancing about him in a circle, hands clasped, his ecstatic brain-trusters sang together the magical incantation, the great emancipating formula: 'WE OWE IT TO OURSELVES!'" (*UL,* 139).

Buckley cites this cartoon as a kind of ideogram of liberal economic dogma. One of the root assumptions of that dogma is that "intellectually, man has come to dominate the economic elements, and that we need only will it, in order to have fair weather all the time" (*UL,* 139). Having made this initial leap of faith, it is relatively easy for the liberal to develop a whole string of corollary myths; one of the most bewitching of which is that of the "spontaneously-generated dollar."

Simply put, the spontaneously generated dollar is that money which is always "there" (proverbially grown on trees) to be spent for worthy public purposes. The government is able to come up with these spontaneously generated dollars by camouflaging the real cost of the services it provides (such as, by financing the subways partially from general revenue rather than entirely from fares) and "by elongating the distance between the place a dollar is collected, and the place where it is spent" (that is, by granting "federal aid") (*UL,* 138). Only a spoilsport would suggest "that the money is *not* 'there' in the sense of being readily available and uncommitted" (*UL,* 141). And it is because nobody wants to be a spoilsport that economic delusion continues until inflation ravages the value of all dollars—not just those created *ex nihilo*.[1]

In a provocative 1975 essay—"For the Inflationists: Mug Shots" (*H,* 220–22)—Buckley quotes Yale president Kingman Brewster on the political causes of inflation. To Brewster, the "inflationary bias of representative government seems . . . the greatest threat to the survival of a democratic political economy." With characteristic modesty, Buckley adds: "That statement is worthy of having been written by, well, myself" (*H,* 220).

The problem lies in the fact that highly mobilized special-interest constituencies encourage spending on particular programs, whereas the advocates of spending restraint are more interested in the aggregate effect of a lawmaker's vote. The dynamics of politics are such that the influence of the latter group is rendered relatively impotent by virtue of its very diffuseness. Focusing on this dilemma, Brewster writes: "Until we can devise ways by which the inflationary consequence of a Congressman's vote is traced to him with the same particularity which attaches to a yea or nay on a revenue bill, we will not cure the disease of public spending motivated by the desire to achieve re-election" (*H,* 221).

As a solution to this problem, Buckley suggests that incumbents who are standing for reelection be required "to list after their names the percentage over revenue for which they voted appropriations, so that, for instance, one would routinely refer to 'Mrs. Bella Abzug (D.–N.Y.– 50)': meaning that she had voted to spend half again as much money as she voted to tax" (*H,* 221–22). One suspects that if ever a candidate is less than eager to supply such information, there will be no shortage of pundits willing to oblige.

As with so many of Buckley's arguments, the case against the spontaneously generated dollar is so inherently cogent that it takes on a life of
its own. One of the more curious political developments of the late 1970s
and early 1980s has been the extent to which liberals and conservatives
have seemed to switch sides on the issue of deficit spending. Perhaps
chastened by economic scarcity or by the electoral backlash against
chronic inflation, all but the most intractable liberals have begun at least
to pay lip service to the notion of a balanced budget. At the same time,
conservatives have discovered a kind of reverse Keynesianism called
"supply-side economics." The theory here is that massive tax cuts will
spontaneously generate revenue. And the size of the deficit really doesn't
matter. Not because "we owe it to ourselves"; but because "a rising tide
lifts all boats."

If the enthusiasm of conservatives for supply-side nostrums fails to
square with their traditional advocacy of balanced budgets, it is because
that advocacy was never categorical. To be sure, in the best of all possible
worlds, there would be no deficits; but those created by a combination of
tax cuts and increased military spending are far more tolerable than any
which result from outlays for social welfare. Are we to conclude, then,
that Buckley and his cohorts are latter-day Marie Antoinettes defending
aristocratic privilege while telling the poor to eat cake? Perhaps. But it is
much more charitable to believe that they are convinced of the efficacy of
laissez-faire and trickle-down economics.

Despite certain populist tendencies in his social and moral opinions,
Buckley is steadfastly libertarian in his economic views. When he is not
attacking liberals for their transgressions, he is defending the rights of
wealth and commerce against the redistributionist impulses of those
same liberals. (Indeed, an entire section of *Execution Eve* is devoted to
"The War on Business and Property.") Nowhere is his case more reso-
nantly made, however, than in the 1967 essay "Let the Rich Alone" (*JE,*
271–76).

Buckley begins his encomium to the well-heeled by chiding the
nonrich for churlish envy of their betters. The rich, he argues, are
indispensable assets to society, "because they . . . are free to turn their
attentions to other matters than getting and spending" (*JE,* 274). "The
function of the rich as risk capitalists," he goes on to say, "is so childishly
easy to understand as to escape the attention of people who can think only
in ideological ellipses. The whole process of capital accumulation begins
by the conception of the surplus. If there is to be civilization, there must
be a surplus, and someone must have control of it. It comes down to the

individual, or the state" (*JE*, 274). Better that wealth be in the hands of H. L. Hunt and J. Paul Getty than under the control of some faceless bureaucrat.

Of course, private largesse—unless it is stuffed into a mattress somewhere—is never exclusively private. Instead, it is "a part of the national patrimony inasmuch as it is constantly at work, supplying credit, employing people, paying tax bills" (*JE*, 275). Rather than excoriating Cole Porter for burning 25,000 candles in a single evening, we should thank him for employing all those candlemakers. And for writing "In the Still of the Night"—which he might not have been able to do without the inspiration of candlelight.

Ultimately, we should judge the rich as individuals, not as members of a class. (Buckley does his part for the cause of evenhandedness by censuring H. L. Hunt for giving capitalism a bad name. Hunt, Buckley suggests, is the moral equivalent of "a tedious socialist of unconventional sexual disposition" whom Winston Churchill said "had managed to 'give sodomy a bad name'" [*JE*, 272].)[2] We can survive the buffoonery of the wealthy just as we have survived "free speech, which means Wayne Morse, and a free press, which means New York *Times* editorials" (*JE*, 275). Indeed, if our society is to remain free, we have no other choice.

The Carrot and the Stick

If the fallacy of the spontaneously generated dollar is essentially a prudential objection to liberal economics, Buckley also harbors more deep-seated philosophical reservations. "The salient economic assumptions of Liberalism," he writes, "are socialist." "They center around the notion that the economic ass can be driven to Point A most speedily by the judicious use of carrot-and-stick, an approach that supersedes the traditional notion of conservatives and classical liberals that we are not to begin with dealing with asses, and that Point A cannot possibly, in a free society, be presumed to be the desired objective of tens of millions of individual human beings" (*UL*, 141).

As appealing as such a statement of principle might be in theory, the actual debate between right and left in the seventies and eighties has not been so much between absolute laissez-faire and socialist paradigms as between different varieties of governmental carrot and stick. If the author of *Up From Liberalism* was the scourge of those who relied on method to effect substantive good, the Buckley of *Four Reforms* was willing to concede that procedural changes might be the most expedient means of rescuing the economic ass from the quagmire into which it had sunk.[3]

Perhaps the most radical of the reforms which Buckley advocates is in the area of taxation. Here, he proposes the replacement of the progressive income tax with a flat 15-percent assessment. Although his philosophical arguments against progressive taxation are too familiar to bear repeating, some of his practical assertions merit detailed consideration.

To begin with, Buckley questions whether the progressivity of the income tax is particularly effective in generating revenue. Traditionally, populists have argued that we should soak the rich for much the same reason that Willie Sutton chose to rob banks: because that's where the money is. And yet, Buckley points out that "91 percent of all taxable income is in brackets of less than $50,000."[4] This being the case, it would seem that—beyond a certain point—progressive taxation is largely punitive.

Although supply-side economics had yet to come into vogue when Buckley wrote *Four Reforms,* he does remind us that tens of billions of dollars "are torturedly spent by people and enterprises attempting to mitigate the steepening incline of progressive taxation" (*FR,* 65). Consequently, the reduction of marginal tax rates would enhance the productive allocation of capital.[5] Moreover, a uniform tax rate would likely divert considerable money from the underground economy. In this regard, Buckley quotes a professor who observed: "Hell, for fifteen percent I wouldn't even *bother* to cheat on my taxes" (*FR,* 82).

Of course, the progressive income tax is not the only impediment to equitable taxation. What we have is a crazy-quilt system of both progressive and regressive taxes. To argue that this is fair is tantamount to saying that a man with one foot in a bucket of ice and the other in a bucket of burning coals is—on balance—comfortable. Buckley addresses this issue by suggesting that the federal government reimburse taxpayers below the poverty line for the effect of regressive federal taxes. (Although he does not specify *how* this should be done, any number of mechanisms could be devised.)[6]

It seems to me that Buckley should be applauded for wanting to relieve low-income taxpayers of the burden of regressive taxation. Unfortunately, he does not go far enough. Even though individuals making less than $2,000 a year in 1968 paid over 50 percent of their incomes in taxes, relatively little of this went to the federal government. Regressive taxes are levied primarily at the state and local level. Any system of tax reform which does not take this fact into consideration must be judged woefully inadequate. Because Buckley is writing as an independent visionary rather than as an agent of the federal government, he has both the right and the duty to propose more comprehensive tax relief for the poor. And, in a rather unconventional way, he claims to do precisely that by advocating elimination of the corporate income tax.

How, you ask, would a tax bonanza for big business help the *lumpen-proletariat?* Well, according to Chairman Bill, the corporation tax is—to a large extent—regressive. Indeed, one study done by the Census Bureau suggests that only two thirds of the cost of corporate taxation falls upon a company's shareholders, while one third is passed along to consumers in the form of higher prices.

By assuming that the split is actually closer to fifty-fifty and by waving his supply-side wand over that datum, Buckley asserts that abolition of the corporation tax would ultimately enhance the federal coffers. He writes: "It is not possible to predict by exactly how much Internal Revenue would benefit from the increased profits to share-holders and increased consumption through lower prices. But . . . one can safely assume, a substantial dollar addition to federal revenues" (*FR,* 77).

Whether or not such an assumption is "safe," is—of course—arguable. However, in the years since Buckley wrote *Four Reforms,* the stick of the corporate income tax has become a carrot in the arsenal of a number of conservative theorists. One of the more innovative notions of the Reagan-Kemp crowd would provide for the establishment of "enter-prise zones"—a policy of federal tax abatements for corporations which would locate in areas of high unemployment. Such taxes cannot be abated, however, if they already have ceased to exist.

In the last analysis, the intellectual value of Buckley's tax proposals should not be underestimated. By thinking the unthinkable, he causes us to reexamine some of our knee-jerk prejudices. Although he may not lead us to the Promised Land, he at least contributes to the dialogue on how to get out of the desert.

From the Cradle to the Grave

Defenders of the marketplace are most adept at devising means for increasing the economic take. Questions of distribution, however, seem not to engage their imagination nearly so much. If a rising tide lifts all boats, the reasoning goes, why bother? Unfortunately, a boat with too many leaks is more likely to be sunk than lifted by a rising tide. All but the most hardened Darwinian must finally admit that it is the responsibility of an enlightened society to help plug some of those leaks. Accordingly, Buckley has concocted his own inimitable brand of waterproofing.

Much of the waste in our current welfare arrangements, he argues, is due to the folly of crisscrossing dollars. Since the federal government cannot provide aid to any citizen without first having raised the money to do so from other citizens (through taxation or by diluting the value of the money supply through inflation), any efficient welfare program must be concerned with shortening the distance between a "public" dollar's source and its destination. It makes no sense, for example, for the federal government to tax the people of a wealthy state, only to return benefits to them—with a brokerage fee subtracted or a political-influence bonus added—in the form of "federal aid." In the interest of both economy and equity, Buckley proposes that: *"Congress shall appropriate funds for social welfare only for the benefit of those states whose per capita income is below the national average"* (FR, 33).

In a federal system in which some states are richer than others, it is reasonable that a few states receive more money from the national government than they pay in taxes, while the vast majority receives less. Buckley simply contends that the net beneficiaries of this process ought to be the poorer states. As things stand now, that is not always the case: political clout frequently counts more than actual need in determining the allocation of "federal" resources. The most expedient means of correcting this anomaly would be to require the wealthier states to finance their own welfare programs by taking them off the national dole.

Generally speaking, liberals oppose such a radical change in the status quo because of their skepticism about the ability of states to assume the fiscal and political responsibility for leadership in social welfare. Such skepticism, however, is largely the result of ideological inertia. Wealthy states which benefit from federal aid do so either by exploiting the revenue base of poorer states or by relying on the ability of the national government to debase the currency through deficit spending. The institution of Buckley's proposal would require those wealthy states to face up to the financial cost of providing necessary services for their poorer citizens, while the political forces which lobby for welfare programs certainly could endeavor to persuade state and local governments of the social cost of not doing so.

From a purely procedural standpoint, there is much to recommend Buckley's approach. However, for that approach to be both humane and equitable, more is needed than simple abandonment of the federal initiative in human services. If lower levels of government continue to finance their operations through regressive taxes, increased welfare at the state and local level is likely to exacerbate tensions between the structurally impoverished and those who are only slightly better off. Thus, greater decentralization of welfare makes tax reform at these lower levels of government all the more imperative. This issue is one to which "new federalists" such as Buckley must ultimately address themselves.

Properly considered, an enlightened policy of welfare reform must involve more than determining who should pay the piper and call the tune. It also requires some notion of what our responsibilities are in the area of communal provision. Once the jurisdictional battles have been fought, we must tackle the substantive issue of what to do with and for the poor. If Buckley's 1965 campaign for Mayor of New York is any indication of what conservatives regard as an adequate response to that question, we're not likely to see municipalized head-start programs any time soon. (Indeed, Murray Kempton wondered if Gotham's huddled masses might not come away from that campaign "with no firm impression except the unwarranted one that the summer after Bill Buckley is sworn in, all able-bodied welfare clients will be summoned to Sharon, Conn., to beat the frogs in the family lily pond so that the Mayor can sleep at night" [*U*, 126].)

If Squire Buckley succeeds in talking more sense about the governmental assault on poverty than many of those whose hearts are constantly bleeding red ink, he does so with a detachment that is not always easy to distinguish from insensitivity. Although his technical observations about various welfare programs are frequently incisive, his appreciation of the human misery which inspired those programs lacks something of what Edmund Burke called the moral imagination. For Buckley, the most sublime economic value surely is freedom. For the wretched of the earth, however, freedom all too often is just another word for nothin' left to lose.

Chapter Six
Justice For All

Except on the anarchist and totalitarian fringes, the most vexing problem for political philosophy is to find a proper balance between freedom and order. Among mainstream ideologies, whether of the left or the right, one looks in vain for paradigmatic simplicity. It is not so much the relative power as it is the legitimate function of government which divides liberals and conservatives. Both view the state as paternalistic, but each harbors a different view of paternal responsibility. For the liberal, government is a perpetually indulgent sugar daddy who bankrolls us from the cradle to the grave, but who lacks the heart to spank us when we are bad. The conservative, however, insists that the state force us to stand on our feet and make us feel the lash of godly reproof.

Ultimately, what is at issue is not whether one's preference is for spoiled or battered children, but whether one's view of human nature comes from the noble savage school of J. J. Rousseau or the savage savage school of Old Testament prophecy. Whether justice is better served by striving for the sort of environment which will condition the lion to lie down with the lamb or by hiring men with chairs and whips to keep the lion at bay.

The White Man's Burden

If—as La Rochefoucauld observed—hypocrisy is the tribute which vice pays to virtue, then, throughout much of our nation's history, platitudes about human equality and racial brotherhood have been the moral equivalent of a twenty-one gun salute—mere ceremonial bombast. (Samuel Johnson was only the first of many to remark on the incongruity of hearing "yelps about liberty from the drivers of Negroes.") Not surprisingly, William Buckley—whose emergence as a national political observer coincided with the rise of the Civil Rights movement—has written provocatively about what Gunnar Myrdal calls the "American Dilemma."

A cursory glance at the six Buckley anthologies tends to confirm the notion that America's obsession with the race issue reached its peak in the 1960s. *Rumbles Left and Right* (1963) includes one essay on the integration controversy, while *The Jeweler's Eye* (1968) and *The Governor Listeth* (1970) devote entire sections to race. The three most recent collections, however, ignore the topic altogether. (When Pat Moynihan had the temerity to suggest that the black revolution was due for a little "benign neglect," the political fallout was so heavy that he was exiled to New Delhi to serve as ambassador to India; and yet, his prediction has proved uncannily correct.) Even if Buckley, along with the rest of the nation, has turned his attention in recent years to other matters, it is instructive to look back at what he once said about America's most intractable social problem.

Entitled "Can We Desegregate, Hesto Presto," the essay in *Rumbles* argues for governmental restraint in enforcing court-ordered integration. In essence, Buckley contends that the substantive advantages of desegregation are too nebulous to justify the social upheaval necessary to impose those advantages on recalcitrant white southerners. Even a social fabric which perpetuates the symbolic injustices of Jim Crow is worth preserving against the ravages of political atavism.

As plausible as Buckley's argument may sound in the abstract, it bears only a tenuous connection with reality. For one thing, by defending stability in the social order, he is not championing Robert E. Lee and Jefferson Davis, but Orval Faubus and Ross Barnett. Although it might have been pleasant to believe such a social order capable of evolutionary progress, the fact remains that in less than a century the South had "progressed" from enslaving blacks to lynching them. Also, to suggest (as Buckley does in *Up From Liberalism*) that ignorant, lower-class blacks should have to earn the right to vote is to make a perversely circular argument. Since the lack of political power was the very thing that had prevented them from gaining educational and social equality, citing those inequalities as reasons for not enfranchising blacks is sort of like blaming the wet pavement for the rain.

Deference to states' rights and community autonomy would, of course, keep the race issue a regional rather than a national problem. Such a strategy had worked well enough with slavery until the Fugitive Slave Act and the Dred Scott decision inextricably implicated Northern whites in the fate of Southern blacks. (It was at that point that the abolition movement really took off, with the publication of *Uncle Tom's Cabin*— itself a response to the Fugitive Slave Act.) However, the withdrawal of Union troops from the South after the Civil War once again denationalized the question of race, allowing it to simmer on the nation's back burner until well after World War II. By that time, television had made it virtually impossible for any section of the country to conceal the seamier aspects of its public policy—especially with inspired showmen like Martin Luther King eager to expose social injustice.

Although no one could justifiably accuse William Buckley of racial bigotry, it is arguable that he places too much value on social stability and too little on social justice. His distrust of political solutions to racial discrimination may be based on nothing more sinister than the conviction that human brotherhood is most likely to be realized when all aristocrats treat their servants as well as the Buckleys treat theirs. That good masters are no adequate safeguard against an inherently unjust system, a lesson which Mrs. Stowe tried to demonstrate in the characters of Mr. Shelby and Augustine St. Clare, is something that Buckley seems not to have learned.

In *The Jeweler's Eye,* Buckley's concern is less with efforts to extend special legal protections to persecuted minorities in the South than with the barbaric actions of rioting minorities in the North. Somewhat ingeniously, he assigns philosophical responsibility for such barbarism to Martin Luther King. Essentially, Buckley regards nonviolent civil disobedience as a contradiction in terms. "An aspect of non-violence," he contends, "is subjugation to the law" (*JE,* 124). When asked in 1970 to assess Dr. King's impact on American history, Buckley observed: "His attempt to sanctify civil disobedience is at least one of his legacies; if it emerges as his principal legacy, then he should certainly be remembered as a bad force." Indeed, the only law that one is justified in breaking is one that, "by more or less settled agreement on the separation of powers since the time of Christ, is ontologically outside the state's jurisdiction" (*I,* 40).

After the cities had cooled down and civil rights had become a fact of life, Buckley turned his attention to the substantive issues of race relations. In so doing, he developed a conservative rationale for positions not ordinarily identified with the American Right. For lack of a better term, this stance might be characterized as Tory benevolence.

One of the more curious phenomena of the late 1960s and early 1970s was the extent to which the New Left and the Old Right came together—ideologically if not tactically—to oppose the conventional liberal preference for centralized government. This philosophical confluence resulted in Buckley's supporting community control in black neighborhoods—a proposal so radical as to be downright reactionary. A practical corollary to this position is the rejection of absolute meritocracy. "[I]n order [for blacks] to exercise power," he writes, "it becomes necessary to permit black people to assume positions for which they are not qualified by conventional standards. . . . To appoint a black teacher because he is black is racist, granted. But we have reached a point in race relations where it becomes desirable to act consciously in such a way as to accede to such demands of the Negro community as are in the least way plausible. Negro control over the education of Negro children would appear to be one of those desirable objectives" (*GL*, 168).

At first glance, it might seem strange for a conservative like Buckley to support reverse discrimination. However, we must remember that belief in meritocracy is a traditionally liberal faith (a fact which may account for the hostility to affirmative action among those old-time liberals who are now called "neo-conservatives").[1] Tories, on the other hand, have always been skeptical of "merit" and have been much more willing to extend special privileges to favored groups. Add a little *noblesse oblige* to this philosophical disposition and you have preferential treatment for the downtrodden. As Garry Wills notes: "conservatives are bound to the concept of 'historic guilt' for racial wrongs, since those who glory in inherited values and traditions must admit accountability for historic wrongs."[2]

Perhaps Buckley's most extreme plea for racial preference came in a January 13, 1970 article in *Look* in which he argued for the election of a Negro president "in 1980 (or thereabouts)" (*GL*, 181). His point is that such a dramatic gesture would be emotionally liberating for black and white alike. Significantly, the therapeutic candidacy would come not from among the national civil rights establishment, but from among "a class of young Negro leaders who work in the ghettos, in economic cooperatives, in straightforward social work, who are arguing that progress is possible within the System" (*GL*, 184).

As we now know, putting a man on the moon by the end of the sixties proved easier than putting a black man in the White House by the end of the seventies. The election of Ronald Reagan in 1980 could hardly have been what Buckley had in mind (even though Dick Gregory contends that "Reagan" pronounced backward is "Nigger"). However, since no black sought the presidency in 1980, Buckley was forced to support the best *white* candidate. What had happened was that America had symbolically dispelled the race issue by electing a white Southern liberal as president in 1976. Rather than regionalize racism by conveniently returning it to the South, the electorate elevated the offending region to national respectability. Bigotry was pronounced neither an American nor a Southern problem, but an historical nightmare which we had indeed overcome.

Crime and Punishment

A conservative, according to former Philadelphia Mayor Frank Rizzo, is a liberal who has been mugged. With the possible exception of its opposition to high taxes, probably no part of the conservative platform appeals more to the general public than its "get-tough" approach to crime. Persons who live in terror of wanton lawbreakers are decidedly unsympathetic to "bleeding-heart liberals" and fastidious civil libertarians who are often seen as apologists for anarchy. Indeed, the failure of antipoverty programs and rehabilitation efforts to reduce or even slow the growth of violent crime tends to lend credence to the notion that some elements of society should be permanently incarcerated if not dispatched to the hereafter. Although Buckley seems to share this view, his thinking is grounded in philosophical reflection which is frequently more subtle than the formulations of strident law-and-order types.

In *Cruising Speed,* he gives us the text of a speech which he delivered on the lecture circuit in 1971. A meditation on the social necessity of repression, this speech relies on the insights of conservative Lincoln scholar Harry V. Jaffa to demonstrate the fallacy of unconditional reverence for civil liberties. Quoting Jaffa, Buckley observes that "'no American statesman ever violated the ordinary maxims of civil liberties more than did Abraham Lincoln, and few seem to have been more careful of them than Jefferson Davis. . . . *Yet the cause for the sake of which the one slighted these maxims was human freedom, while the other, claiming to defend the forms of constitutional government, found in those forms a ground for defending and preserving human slavery'"* (*CS,* 199).

Buckley's point is that the concept of civil rights and civil liberties presupposes the existence of a civil order. Although these rights and liberties may be morally grounded in nature, they can become concrete actualities only in a society strong enough to repress those who threaten the safety and property of their neighbors. The fact that some criminals are motivated by political impulses does not excuse their antisocial behavior. Nor will historical appeals to our nation's revolutionary tradition suffice. Commenting on our war for independence, Buckley writes: "I do not find anywhere in the informed literature of that period any suggestion that it was other than the accepted right of the British throne to resist the American revolution" (*CS,* 205).

It is difficult to quarrel with the assertion that a government has the institutional imperative to defend itself against violent overthrow and that in time of armed insurrection (such as the Civil War) conventional legal protections may need to be suspended. What is insidious about this argument, however, is Buckley's eagerness to invoke emergency expedients in more normal times. Just because the New Left desired the overthrow of the American government and occasionally used violent and illegal means in pursuit of that end does not prove that it posed as great a threat to the nation as did the Confederate rebellion. Excessive or extraconstitutional repression can be justified in only the most extreme circumstances. For the most part, such circumstances did not obtain in the political uprisings of the sixties and early seventies. Indeed, as a practical matter, police overreaction (as in Chicago in 1968) was counterproductive in that it won sympathy for demonstrators who might otherwise have been ignored.

In all fairness, it should be pointed out that Buckley is not arguing for suspension of the Bill of Rights even for the likes of Jerry Rubin (who is now an investment counsellor, anyway). Rather, he is suggesting that it is possible for men of good will and stern morality to interpret constitutional guarantees somewhat differently than have the Warren Court and the American Civil Liberties Union. It has become one of the unquestioned axioms of Western jurisprudence that it is better for ten guilty men to go free than for one innocent man to be convicted; and yet, such a principle cannot be extended indefinitely. Otherwise, as Buckley notes, we would be committed to "the simple act of ceasing to prosecute anyone" (*FR,* 120). Does the ever-decreasing ratio of convictions to crimes committed prove that defendants are now being treated more fairly than in previous eras or only that the art of legal gamesmanship has reached a higher level of sophistication?

In *Four Reforms,* Buckley cites the incontestable thesis of Sidney Hook's *The Paradoxes of Freedom,* namely, that "the extension of any single right to infinite length almost necessarily gets in the way of other rights, infinitely extended. . . . How does one achieve, simultaneously, a totally free press, and a totally fair trial? How can one absolutize the Fifth Amendment's guarantee against self incrimination, and the Sixth Amendment's guarantee of the right to compel testimony?" Buckley concludes that "it is the job of the judiciary, building on the law, to reconcile rights, rather than to draw any single right out to lengths so extreme as to unbalance the structure" (*FR,* 121).

Specifically, Buckley argues that the Fifth Amendment should be construed not as a protection against the *possibility* of incriminating oneself but against the *requirement* to do so. It is one thing to prohibit torture, quite another to exclude evidence that is obtained by unsportsmanlike conduct. The exclusionary rule, as it is presently applied, serves to punish the overzealous policeman or prosecutor by denying certain evidence to the jury. "Free the defendant. . . , and you deprive the constable of the platonic satisfaction he'd have taken from a conviction. But his punishment is more nearly like the athlete's whom the referee rules as having been offside" (*FR,* 127). However, the real losers in this "game" are not the constables in question, but the once and future victims of the freed criminal.

In addition to redefining the scope of the Fifth Amendment, Buckley proposes several other reforms. These include such old standards as reducing judicial paperwork and decriminalizing "victimless" offenses. Another idea that is not as frequently heard would abolish the much-abused grand jury system and require the prosecution to disclose its case to the defense prior to trial. This latter reform would make the guilty defendant all the more likely to plead guilty and would allow the innocent one to prepare a more adequate defense.

Since the adversary system of justice is more a contest of wits between attorneys for the prosecution and the defense than an impartial quest for truth, it is absurd to regard the procedures of this contest as sacrosanct. Even precious constitutional freedoms are relative matters whose operative meaning changes with each new Supreme Court decision. Thus, Buckley's willingness to reexamine some of our cherished shibboleths is both daring and refreshing. Ultimately, he reminds us, we must distinguish between the state "when it is acting as agent for its own aggrandizement, and . . . when it is acting in behalf of an aggrieved citizen" (*FR,* 125). In the latter case, knee-jerk antistatists are not striking out so much against Big Brother as against his defenseless siblings.

Assuming that these procedural reforms would enable us to apprehend and convict many more lawbreakers than is presently the case, the question remains—what are we to do with them? In recent years, something of a national consensus seems to have emerged—or reemerged—for inflicting the ultimate penalty on those who have committed premeditated murder. Although Buckley has not been in the forefront of those urging restoration of capital punishment, he presents some of the main arguments for that position in an essay contained—quite appropriately—in *Execution Eve* (401–3).

Buckley organizes his discussion—which is actually a summary of the case made by Ernest van den Haag— around a refutation of some of the weaker objections raised by opponents of the death penalty. To begin with, he demonstrates that unfair administration of capital punishment is not a compelling argument against the sanction itself. Since *any* punishment can be inequitably applied against the poor and the black, we should strive for more evenhanded administration of justice rather than for elimination of the death penalty. Moreover, the fact that executions occur with relative infrequency may well suggest that the process ought to be expedited not scrapped. Prisoners languish on death row because of a concern for their rights, not because the state desires that they should suffer "unusual" punishment. Nor is the death penalty "cruel" in the sense of being painfully inflicted or manifestly undeserved.

Surely, the least tenable argument against capital punishment is that it fails to deter capital crimes. The fact is that we cannot know with any certainty how many potential murderers are discouraged by the threat of possible execution. Given such uncertainty, is it not more reasonable to risk sacrificing the lives of the guilty than endangering the safety of the innocent?

Because Buckley's position is ultimately based on the possible deterrent effect of capital punishment, we ought to examine that argument more closely. A moment's reflection suggests that we open a can of worms when we seek to justify a given penalty solely because it would result in the preservation of innocent lives. Since more innocent persons are killed by reckless drivers than by murderers, those who are categorically committed to saving innocent lives ought to argue for the execution—or at least the permanent incarceration—of reckless drivers.[3] This argument is not made because most people realize that such a punishment would be vastly disproportionate to the crime in question.[4]

After all the ancillary arguments are dispensed with, the question finally remains whether death is an appropriate punishment for murder. Those who contend that it is subscribe to a retributive notion of justice. The death penalty came into being as a socially acceptable means of achieving revenge for the most serious crime that it is possible to commit. Thus, the controversy over capital punishment ultimately comes down to a subjective judgment about the moral validity of taking a life for a life. One wishes that Buckley would have addressed himself to this question rather than to lesser issues.

If Buckley's position on capital punishment is what one might expect from a prominent conservative, his stand on marijuana clearly is not.[5] With the possible exception of his support for the Panama Canal treaties, his endorsement of removing criminal penalties for possession of marijuana probably has created more dismay within the conservative community than anything else he has ever done. On this issue, the instincts of the libertarian prevail over those of the lion tamer.

Although he is reputed to have sampled the illegal weed after his yacht was safely past the twelve-mile limit, Buckley does not recommend its use. Rather, his point is that the current pot sanctions are excessive. Smoking marijuana may make little sense, but putting the smoker in a place like Attica makes even less. Because very few people actually desire to see the jails filled with otherwise law-abiding potheads, those who urge retaining felony status for marijuana possession are engaged in a dangerous hypocrisy.

The change in public attitudes toward pot came about at approximately the same time as the sons and daughters of middle America began experimenting with the drug. As long as marijuana was used primarily by blacks and bohemian types, it had about as much chance as bestiality of being legalized. However, when the teenage offspring of some of America's most prominent families were busted and let off with a reprimand, it became clear that the times they were a changin'.

If we have arrived at a national consensus that the more draconian marijuana laws ought not to be enforced, then it is absurd to keep them on the books. To send one in a thousand users to the penitentiary may be statistically insignificant, but that is little consolation if you are the unlucky one. Also, given the epidemic increase in violent crime, it seems a profligate waste of judicial resources to crowd the courts and prisons further by piling on even a handful of marijuana offenders.

To decriminalize marijuana possession would be to treat it in much the same way that booze was treated during Prohibition and that gambling, prostitution, and pornography are treated today—the peddler is imprisoned, while the patron is treated much less harshly. That such a solution should be preferable to outright legalization makes more sense politically than logically. Given the stigma which marijuana still carries in some quarters and the paucity of precise scientific knowledge about its effects, the country probably is not ready for pot at the Automat. That particular consensus is still a long way off. And the average politician survives by never being ahead of his time.

Another area in which Buckley distances himself from some of the more primitive impulses of the right is prison reform. As he noted in January 1967: "The conservative is hardly opposed to the devising of means by which human beings can be rehabilitated. He has opposed, rather, the notion that society's debts to the criminal are requited by letting him alone to vent his resentments against innocent people" (*JE*, 178). In other words, it is possible to desire that criminals be punished without necessarily wanting to see them subjected to gratuitous violence, homosexual rape, and generally intolerable living conditions. Since most prisoners will eventually be released, a prudent society does well to consider what sort of product the system is putting back on the streets.

A conservative penology must begin with the notion that criminals behave as they do because they have freely chosen an antisocial life-style. They are not likely to be reformed by listening to liberal psychiatrists and sociologists tell them that they are not really to blame for their actions. What is needed is "deliberate conversion . . . to a more responsible lifestyle."[6] This, in the opinion of Buckley and Watergate conspirator-turned-penal reformer Charles Colson, is best accomplished through a religious conversion.

While Colson and his cohorts are attempting to improve the spiritual condition of prisoners, there is much that society can do to improve their physical surroundings. With only two of every one hundred crimes resulting in imprisonment and our prisons already overcrowded by some 200,000 inmates, any progress in the apprehension and conviction of criminals is likely only to exacerbate the hideously cramped conditions which presently make our penitentiaries into jungles. The answer, however, is not to build more jails (even assuming that a tax-weary public could be persuaded to pay for them). Rather, the prisons should be emptied of those offenders who pose no physical danger to society.

There are cheaper and more constructive ways of dealing with non-dangerous criminals than tossing them into the slammer. An inmate who served time with Colson, for example, had once been chairman of the board of trustees of the American Medical Association. Society surely would be better served by requiring that man to render free medical care to the needy than by spending $20,000 a year to keep him locked up and working in the prison laundry.

Although nonincarcerative punishment for nondangerous offenders would be of obvious benefit both to the offenders themselves and to society in general, less obvious benefits would accrue to the violent few (approximately half of the present prison population) who remain behind bars. They would now be relieved of overcrowding and the horrors which go with it. Under such conditions, rehabilitation might even have a chance to succeed. Lester Maddox had the sequence reversed when he said that to improve the quality of prisons we must first get a better class of prisoners.

Chapter Seven

The Unmaking of New York

In commenting on Norman Mailer's 1969 campaign for Mayor of New York, Russell Baker writes: "the idea of a literate man holding public office is so outrageous these days that when one announces he would like to try, everybody suspects him of joking."[1] One need only consider William Buckley's experience in running four years earlier for the same office to which Mailer aspired to realize the truth of Baker's statement.[2] Indeed, we seem to live in an era in which the public profoundly distrusts literate politicians.

It may well be that, contrary to the popular wisdom, we do not now suffer so much from an excess as from a lack of political rhetoric. While the nation's nominal literacy has increased spectacularly over the past two centuries, its leaders have become progressively less articulate. To compare the Federalist Papers or the speeches of Abraham Lincoln with the solecisms of our contemporary office-holders is to conclude—with Henry Adams—that Darwin was wrong.

Although Shelley may have been overstating his case when he declared poets to be "the unacknowledged legislators of the world," it is true that the literary imagination can occasionally bring a fresh and useful perspective to political affairs. As an outsider, Buckley was able to say things which his opponents would not have dared to utter. As a master stylist, he said these things in an aesthetically memorable way. We are fortunate to have Buckley's own account of his singular foray into electoral politics in a thoroughly fascinating narrative called *The Unmaking of a Mayor*.

A Choice Not an Echo

To understand what William F. Buckley was trying to accomplish in his 1965 race for the New York mayoralty, it is helpful to recall the low standing which conservatism enjoyed at that time both in the nation at large and in the state of New York in particular. The previous year Barry Goldwater had suffered a landslide defeat at the hands of Lyndon Johnson and, in so doing, had failed to win the support of the top four Republicans in New York State—Governor Nelson Rockefeller, senators Jacob Javits and Kenneth Keating, and Manhattan Congressman John V. Lindsay. That same John V. Lindsay was now proposing to run for Mayor of New York. If not stopped there, he was likely to be catapulted into national prominence, from whence he could lead a liberal takeover of the GOP.

In New York the Republican Party already was considerably more liberal than in the nation as a whole. From Theodore Roosevelt to Fiorello La Guardia to Nelson Rockefeller the progressive wing of the GOP traditionally has been led by politicians from New York. At the same time, the state's active and influential Liberal Party kept the Democrats from straying too far to the right. As a result, New York conservatives were effectively frozen out of the electoral process.

In an effort to combat this disenfranchisement, two Buckley allies—J. Daniel Mahoney and Kieran O'Doherty—founded the New York State Conservative Party. The purpose of this new party was not to supplant but to influence the GOP, to exercise leverage on the Republicans similar to that of the Liberal Party on the Democrats. Had there been no Liberal Party, Buckley asserts, there would have been no need for a countervailing conservative insurgency.

The Conservative Party came into being in 1961 and ran statewide candidates in 1962 and 1964. However, it was not until 1965 that the new movement had an opportunity to run a candidate for Mayor of New York. Since he was—next to Barry Goldwater—the most prominent conservative spokesman in America, William Buckley seemed an attractive nominee. Although he lived in Connecticut, the fact that he maintained a residence in New York made him eligible to run for municipal office. Besides, with Bobby Kennedy as their junior senator, New Yorkers were used to celebrity carpetbaggers.

From the outset it was clear that Buckley's campaign had two principal objectives: to propose concrete solutions to the problems facing the city and to halt the political ascendancy of John Lindsay. Regrettably, the press concentrated far too much on the second of these objectives while virtually ignoring the first. The two were closely related, however; for Buckley regarded the defeat of Lindsay to be less a personal matter than an ideological imperative. He saw Lindsay as being as much an anomaly among Republicans as George Wallace was among Democrats. What was at stake was nothing less than the continued existence of an identifiable two-party system.

Lindsay's claim to be a Republican was, according to Buckley, "largely . . . a matter of baptismal affirmation" (*U,* 69). That affirmation, however, had been ratified by New York's Seventeenth Congressional District, which sent Lindsay to Washington four times with ever-increasing margins of victory (71.5 percent of the vote in 1964). His success gladdened the hearts of liberals seeking philosophical hegemony within the political system. (In chiding Harry Golden for his refusal to support Lindsay's mayoral bid, David Dubinsky noted that the election of Lindsay would prove "that the way for a Republican to get elected is to act like Lindsay" [*U*, 73].) Moreover, in the wake of the Goldwater debacle, the GOP was particularly receptive to new faces and to new ideas. Back home, the mediagenic Lindsay already was being billed as "The District's Pride— The Nation's Hope."

The Seventeenth District, though marginally Democratic in registration, had a habit of sending Republicans to Congress. (Lindsay was only one in a long line stretching back to Bruce Barton in the 1930s.)[3] Sometimes known as the "silk stocking" district, Lindsay's home ground sheltered "not only just about all the resident financial, social, and artistic elite of New York but also probably the densest national concentration of vegetarians, pacifists, hermaphrodites, junkies, Communists, Randites, clam-juice-and-betel-nut eaters; plus, also, a sprinkling of quite normal people" (*U*, 70–71). By and large, these were not the sort of folks you would expect to find attending the Rotary in Peoria.

Early on in *The Unmaking of a Mayor,* Buckley documents Lindsay's political heterodoxy by analyzing his congressional voting record. To infer that Lindsay was the George Wallace of the Republican Left solely from his high ADA rating, however, is somewhat specious. Wallace was a thorn in the side of the Democratic Party not because of his heretical opinions, but because of his histrionic opposition to the policies of two Democratic presidents. It was not until the Nixon years that Lindsay would mount a similar offensive within the GOP.

It is wishful thinking on Buckley's part to argue that in 1965 Lindsay was opposing the settled body of Republican opinion. For at that time there was no such body of opinion. The factions of the party to which Buckley and Lindsay belonged were engaged in a struggle for the soul of the GOP. (Wallace was a remnant of a similar struggle waged by the Democrats in 1948.) As a mere gadfly, Lindsay could have been tolerated. As the possible "wave of the future," he had to be stopped.

Like many politicians, Lindsay was adept at historical name-dropping. His particular patron saint was Abraham Lincoln, "toward whom Mr. Lindsay tends to refer all questions having to do with the nature of the Republican Party" (*U*, 84). And yet, if the GOP bills itself as the "party of Lincoln," what can we conclude about that party other than the fact that it probably opposes a reinstitution of chattel slavery? With the aid of Lincoln scholar and Goldwater advisor Harry V. Jaffa, Buckley ponders the philosophical legacy of our sixteenth president.

In the light of such historical scrutiny, Lindsay's comments on Lincoln reveal a mixture of sentimentality, ignorance, and wishful thinking. Whatever else he may have been, Lincoln was not a twentieth-century liberal. Although he was an heroic opponent of slavery, he was also an advocate of white supremacy. Although he fought to preserve constitutional government, no president in American history violated civil liberties more consistently than did Lincoln. Moreover, Honest Abe's economic views are at embarrassing variance with the welfare-state prescriptions of Mr. Lindsay.[4] The similarities between these two men ultimately seem less philosophic than biological. Lindsay was Lincolnian only in being of above-average height.

Buckley concludes his preliminary discussion of Lindsay with an examination of the latter's rhetorical style. Although he had not read George Orwell's "Politics and the English Language," Buckley shared Orwell's insight that "political chaos is connected with the decay of language."[5] Thus, it is a legitimate—if depressing—activity to scrutinize the ways in which a politician chooses to communicate his thought.

Lindsay's speeches and magazine articles, we are told by his biographer D. E. Button, "have habitually been pounded out by Lindsay himself in the recesses of a den at home; until the multispeech demands of the mayoralty there was no 'Lindsay-writer.'"[6] Upon discovering this fact, Buckley sighs: "I feared as much" (U, 90). "I would not bring up the matter," he continues, "except that I have come to believe that Mr. Lindsay's rhetoric bears on his politics; indeed that his rhetoric is an expression of his nature. . . . Mr. Lindsay has a real flair for politics . . . ; he has none at all for self-expression: or, perhaps more accurately, he has absolutely perfect powers of self-expression" (U, 91).

As Buckley sees it, Lindsay's rhetorical sins fall into two categories: (1) an inflated use of the first-person singular; and (2) an affinity for "extra-personal clichés, the profligate use of which suggests the failure of the observer himself to recognize the uniqueness he is nevertheless trying to stress" (U, 95).

In the first of these categories we find this gem: "'I will defend as long as I have a voice in my body' the jurisdiction of the Supreme Court . . . on an occasion when there was never any possibility that the voice in his body might serve as the last line of defense between the Supreme Court and the barbarians" (U, 94). And this one: "'As long as I have a voice in my body, I will speak for what I believe is right'—referring to things in general. Once again, the salvific voice, an appropriate context for the use of which it is difficult to conceive, save possibly as a caption to Michelangelo's drawing of God breathing life into Adam" (*U*, 95).

Rising from pomposity to mere banality, "Lindsay volunteered the insight [in opposition to an antipornography bill]: 'Must we burn down the barn in order to catch the rat?' (The answer depends, of course, on one's relative attachment to the survival of the barn, and the death of the rat; as Captain Ahab would have observed)" (*U*, 95).

In a sense these rhetorical habits—and Buckley cites several more examples of each—bespeak a supreme self-confidence bordering on egomania. The man who prefers his own flat, cliché-ridden prose to the more graceful formulations of his hired speechwriters is precisely the sort who would see himself as a municipal (or national) Messiah. Such a role is hazardous indeed for those of us unable to walk on water.

The Guts to Tell the Truth

At the time he launched his candidacy, Buckley saw New York as a city bent on the appeasement of various voting blocs. By approaching government in this piecemeal, incremental fashion, politicians managed to get elected but also to formulate policies which—by virtue of their incoherence—rendered life in the city increasingly intolerable.

Consider, for example, the plight of a not atypical New Yorker:

A modern Justine *could*, in New York City, wake up in the morning in a room she shares with her unemployed husband and two children, crowd into a subway in which she is hardly able to breathe, disembark at Grand Central and take a crosstown bus which takes twenty minutes to go the ten blocks to her textile loft, work a full day and receive her paycheck from which a sizeable deduction is withdrawn in taxes and union fees, return via the same ordeal, prepare supper for her family and tune up the radio to full blast to shield the children from the gamy denunciations her next door neighbor is hurling at her husband. . . .

The litany of misfortune continues as Justine walks to the neighborhood park for a little fresh air, only to fall into a coughing fit as "the sulphur dioxide excites her latent asthma." She arrives back home, after losing her handbag to a purse-snatcher, and proceeds to oversee her son's homework. Although the lad recently had spent his fourteenth birthday in the company of a well-known pusher, Justine discovers that he is not at all familiar with the alphabet. "She hauls off and smacks him, but he dodges and she bangs her head against the table. The ambulance is slow in coming and at the hospital there is no doctor in attendance. An intern finally materializes and sticks her with a shot of morphine, and she dozes off to sleep. And dreams of John Lindsay" (*U,* 32).

In seeking to alleviate the plight of all New York's Justines, Buckley offered a program which began by recognizing the finite nature of the city's resources. Although he was not an advocate of the "small is beautiful" philosophy, he felt that New York's unnatural obsession with size had caused the city to overextend itself in a number of areas. Of course, to make this observation was to risk offending those key voting blocs which John Lindsay and his Democratic opponent Abraham Beame needed to flatter in order to win election. Thus, Buckley was the only candidate in the race who—in the words of his own campaign slogan—had "the guts to tell the truth."

In his position papers on water usage and industrial pollution, the Conservative Party candidate showed definite conservationist tendencies. The problem of maintaining an adequate water supply was a timely issue in New York, since the city was then experiencing a temporary but critical water shortage. Accordingly, Buckley recommended that New York follow the lead of other cities and institute water metering. The rates would fluctuate in relation to supply in such a way as to discourage waste. His approach to air and water pollution, as outlined in a thirteen-point program, involved a similar carrot-and-stick policy toward private industry: fines would be levied against excessive polluters and tax credits extended to firms seeking to clean up their act.

It was in dealing with traffic, however, that Buckley courted his broadest range of political unpopularity. His proposals included charging tolls on cars registered outside the city which sought to enter Manhattan during peak hours; staggering the days on which trucks would be allowed to deliver nonperishable goods to certain parts of the city; and raising transit fares to reflect the genuine cost of public transportation. And yet, the suggestion which probably received the most attention—albeit in the form of derision—was that the city construct a bikeway to expedite travel and to help its citizens improve their muscle tone.

The issue of municipal finances also raises the question of how to live within realistic limits. Buckley's ideas for restoring New York to fiscal soundness involved reforms in such related areas as welfare and taxation. Beyond these, however, the prospective mayor insisted upon a certain measure of economic sobriety. The city should cease its borrow-now-pay-later philosophy and its leaders should resist the temptation to disguise the actual cost of government services. Moreover, he felt it essential that the federal government reduce taxes so that money would be available to local authorities to finance local programs. It made little sense to Buckley for the central government to take the peoples' money from them, route it through Washington, and then return it minus a federal brokerage fee.

In his position paper on taxation Buckley bemoaned the administrative burden created by a confusing thicket of city taxes. Would it not make more sense, he asked, to replace those various levies with a single value-added tax? Such a policy seemed to be working well in Western Europe and it had the advantage of generating revenues from a broad tax base while reducing "the problem of policing business taxes to that of merely verifying cash receipts and cash expenditures" (*U,* 219).

Education was another area in which Buckley argued for what he considered a commonsense approach. He defended the concept of the neighborhood school, advocated more remedial instruction, and urged stricter discipline and more rigorous academic standards. He also supported decentralized administration of the school system and greater community control. Although these positions were originally attacked as racist, many of them subsequently have come to be adopted by thoughtful black leaders. The candidate was also ahead of his time in insisting on the payment of tuition by those students in the city university system who could afford to do so. This was one of the demands made by the federal government when it bailed out the indigent city a decade later.

In addressing himself to the housing problem in New York City, Buckley argued against the scorched-earth policy known as urban renewal. As an alternative, he advocated the renovation of existing housing. Although government would need to play some role in this renovation, private initiative would be encouraged through reforming the tax structure and reducing the power of monopoly labor unions. Finally, the Conservative platform supported the phased elimination of rent controls. Such controls contributed to the housing shortage while benefitting real estate speculators and wealthy slum lords at the expense of honest property owners.

It is not necessary to dwell at length on Buckley's positions in regard to crime and narcotics. Suffice it to say that here he took the "get-tough" stance typical of the right wing. He advocated hiring additional police, abolishing the Civilian Review Board, tightening parole and probation standards, and indemnifying victims of certain crimes. In regard to narcotics, he gave some initial consideration to the British system of supplying heroin addicts with their daily fix, but eventually came out for the quarantining of those addicts. Addiction is a contagious disease, he reasoned, and one which the government must treat as it would a plague.

Unquestionably, the most virulent criticism of Buckley was engendered by his stance on welfare. In addition to demanding that welfare clients be available for work on public projects and that frauds be purged from the Aid to Dependent Children program, the Conservative platform urged a one-year residency requirement for welfare applicants and a program to support chronic welfare cases outside the city limits. The last proposal was meant to alleviate overcrowding in the city and to remove some on the public dole to areas where they could be supported more cheaply.

Rather than focusing on the practical difficulties of such a policy, Buckley's political opponents—a group which included significant portions of the press—accused him of proposing concentration camps for welfare recipients. The implication here was that the Conservative candidate was what Gore Vidal would later brand him—a "crypto-Nazi." The fact that these same people never characterized Franklin Roosevelt's Civilian Conservation Corps as a slave-labor program tells us less about Buckley or Roosevelt than it does about the mind set of certain ideological vigilantes.

The Candidate and His Critics

When a nonpolitician decides to seek public office, those very qualities which have made him successful in his original line of work may suddenly prove to be liabilities.[7] This certainly was the case for mayoral candidate Bill Buckley. His urbane manner and rhetorical flamboyance, along with his refusal to observe the more unctuous rituals of campaigning, made him seem aloof and pompous. Also, the subtleties of his dialectic were all but lost on an electorate habituated to simplistic thought and utterance. And finally, his wit called into question the seriousness of his effort.

Buckley's first press conference set the tone for his ensuing campaign. According to Murray Kempton, the candidate "read his statement of principles in a tone for all the world that of an Edwardian resident commissioner reading aloud the 39 articles of the Anglican establishment to a conscript assemblage of Zulus" (U, 126). He declined to make specifically ethnic appeals or to campaign in the ingratiating way of conventional politicians. Asked how many votes he expected to get, Buckley replied: "conservatively speaking, one"; and quizzed about what he would do if elected, he responded: "demand a recount."

Much of the charm of *The Unmaking of a Mayor* derives from the fact that Buckley is describing a process in which he was himself a participant. In this sense, the book is at least on the fringes of "new journalism." Although he lacks the skills at narrative and characterization which one finds in the best work of Mailer, Capote, and Wolfe, Buckley partially compensates by giving us a work of great polemical pace and intensity. The persona which he projects is not that of a grim ideologue, however, but of a sportsman who loves competition for its own sake. For this reason, he was able to tolerate—and even welcome—philosophical opposition. What he could not countenance was incivility or foul play. Unfortunately, he experienced plenty of both in the political arena.

Buckley prefaces *Mayor* with an account of the rough treatment he received from the press and some public figures because of a speech he gave prior to his campaign. The speech in question was delivered before a Communion Breakfast of Roman Catholic policemen and dealt with the inadequacy of public appreciation for our boys in blue. Buckley, however, was somewhat indiscreet in his choice of examples.

A month earlier the police in Selma, Alabama, had distinguished themselves by beating up a group of civil rights demonstrators. Although he acknowledged the excesses of the Selma cops, Buckley also chided the television networks for not making it clear that those cops had waited twenty minutes between ordering the demonstrators to disperse and moving in on them: "the policemen moved, excitedly, humanly, forward: excessively, yes, and their excesses on that day have been rightly criticized, but were ever the excesses criticized of those who provoked them beyond the endurance that we tend to think of as human?" (*U,* 13).

Press accounts of this address ignored Buckley's reservations about the behavior of the Selma police and reported that applause and laughter greeted his reference to the fate of Mrs. Viola Liuzzo, the Detroit housewife who had been murdered as a result of her participation in the Selma demonstrations. A tape of the speech, however, recorded the qualifying context of Buckley's remarks while indicating no laughter or applause where such responses were alleged to have transpired. The irresponsibility, if not the malice, of the press is thus exposed.

In the process of this exposure, though, Buckley makes some strategic miscalculations. To begin with, he reveals an almost categorical insensitivity to the issue of police brutality. (He admits in a footnote to having later discovered that the heroic restraint of Selma's finest was closer to four than to twenty minutes, but apparently fails to realize that this factual contingency undercuts the basis of his original argument.) As a result, he tends to alienate the reader who must either adore the Selma police or possess the fair-mindedness of Voltaire to be more than technically outraged at the criticism Buckley received. It seems that he could have addressed himself to a somewhat wider audience.

Although the candidate was plagued by a bad press throughout the campaign, he received some favorable notices from commentators like Murray Kempton of the *New York Post*, Theodore H. White of *Life*, and Norman Mailer of the *Village Voice*. ("The biggest boost to his campaign," Buckley claimed at one point, was "a letter from Mailer promising not to support him.")[8] He even won the long-distance endorsement of that redoubtable California liberal Groucho Marx.[9]

Denounced as he was by the editorial powers that be, Buckley eventually earned the respect of the working press—if only because he made their jobs a little less dull. Indeed, a free-lance writer told the candidate that "a senior editor of *The New York Times* confessed . . . that he had taken to dispatching different reporters to" Buckley's "press conferences, because 'everyone who came back after a couple of them said he was going to vote for the son of a bitch'" (*U,* 304). Like heroin addiction, Buckleyism is apparently contagious.

The Best Laid Plans

As things turned out the Conservative candidate finished with 13.4 percent of the total vote; while Beame got 38.8 percent and Lindsay 45.3 percent. Had Buckley not been in the race, it is conceivable that Beame would have won some conservative votes. Indeed, his presumed ability to add and subtract figures caused Beame to be perceived as marginally less liberal than Lindsay (a fact which won Lindsay the endorsement of the Liberal Party to supplement that of the GOP).

In practical terms, then, Buckley's campaign failed to achieve one of its major objectives—the defeat of John Lindsay—and may well have been instrumental in accomplishing the opposite. However, in pursuing its other principal goal—to tell the truth about the city without regard to political consequences—the campaign was somewhat more successful. Buckley spoke the truth as he understood it to be and he did suffer the political consequences. Still, it would be wrong to infer too much from the fact of his defeat. We must first consider what he had going against him.

Although currently a significant political force, the New York State Conservative Party was a fledgling venture in 1965. Also, Buckley was running in perhaps the most liberal city of a country which had overwhelmingly rejected doctrinaire conservatism in its presidential election the previous year. Because he was given no chance of winning (an impression which the candidate did little to dispel), the majority of voters looked upon him as a curiosity and a spoiler. As Norman Mailer's campaign manager Joe Flaherty noted, "most men take their politics very lightly and their politicians very seriously."[10] Consequently, the public tends to ignore even the best ideas of a sure loser.

It would have been interesting to observe the public's response to Buckley in a race that he stood some chance of winning. The 1969 mayoral election might have provided such an opportunity, for political conditions had changed drastically by then. The nation had moved far enough to the right to elect Richard Nixon president in 1968[11] and the city's honeymoon with Lindsay had long since ended. The Conservative Party's mayoral candidate—State Senator John Marchi—challenged and defeated Lindsay in the Republican primary. Had Buckley run instead of Marchi, it is reasonable to assume that he, too, would have beaten Lindsay. Even if he had gone on to lose the general election,[12] the press and the political establishment would have been forced to take Buckley seriously in a way that they did not have to in 1965.

If Buckley's 1965 campaign had done no more than produce *The Unmaking of a Mayor*, it still would have been worth the effort. What it did beyond that was to foretell the unmaking of New York. By refusing to live within the limits which reality defined and Buckley identified, the city overspent and mismanaged its way into virtual bankruptcy. Whether the election of New York's Cassandra would have averted catastrophe is hard to say. What we can say with reasonable conviction is that William Buckley tried to bring some much needed clarity of thought to the political process. We can also say of him what Buckley himself once said of Adlai Stevenson: that he "was devoted to a means of communicating his thought to the people, which, because it was based on the assumption of human intelligence, was, therefore, based on the assumption of human nobility" (*JE*, 305).

Chapter Eight
Teacher's Pest

William Buckley began his career as an educational critic when—as a small boy—he crashed a teacher's meeting at the private school in which he was enrolled and "proceeded to expound to the stunned faculty on the virtues of isolationism, the dignity of the Catholic Church, and the political ignorance of the school staff."[1] He has been going strong ever since.

Gladly Would He Teach

All six of Buckley's anthologies contain essays dealing with education, the campuses, or simply "the kids." As one might expect, many of the selections from the late 1960s and early 1970s focus on the political disruptions of that era. Because their author's reactions to this phenomenon are fairly predictable, we need not dwell on them here. A glance at his account of giving the 1970 commencement address at "a very large university in California" should suffice to give us a flavor of the times and a sense of the great strides made by God and Man in the two decades since Buckley's own graduation (*I*, 232–34).

To begin with, there was such vocal opposition to the selection of the speaker that the chancellor of the university showed exceptional courage in not withdrawing the invitation. Just prior to the speech, the president of the student body announced that several of the graduates had "a presentation to make to Mr. Buckley." This turned out to be a cardboard box containing a small pig.

Slipping away from its intended recipient, "the pig went off towards the podium, where the Chancellor was by this time reading the accomplishments of a young man who was standing up there to get his scholarship. But at that moment the pig began to urinate right by the Chancellor, and nobody paid any attention to the student who had worked very hard for a couple of years to distinguish himself" (*I*, 233).

When time for the main event finally arrived, "I spoke uninterruptedly, if you don't count a dozen students filing out, and one smoke bomb that sort of fizzled off in the wrong direction" (*I*, 233). "You get to wondering," Buckley concludes, "whether, in the old phrase, you're playing horse to other people's Lady Godiva" (*I*, 234).

What are perhaps his greatest heights of invective against student barbarism are those Buckley reaches at the expense of a Los Angeles adolescent named Rickie Ivie (*GL*, 393–95). A spokesman for the black revolution, Ivie railed against his high school's attempts to inculcate "middle-class values" in its students. "An example of that training is the inclusion in the curriculum of the music of Johann Sebastian Bach. The venerable composer is described by Master Ivie as 'that old dead punk'" (*GL*, 394).

Rising to the defense of his idol, amateur harpsichordist Buckley fumes: "To call the greatest genius who ever lived an 'old, dead punk,' . . . is not so much contemptible as pitiable: conducive of that kind of separation one feels from animals, rather than from other human beings. . . . if Bach is a punk, then the human dislocation is total, and nothing at all is worth striving after, not peace, or freedom, or good relations between the races" (*GL*, 394, 95). Thus, does a juvenile ideologue achieve unwarranted fame by taking his place in Buckley's modern *Dunciad*.

It should not be assumed, however, that the educational system is beyond hope. In *Four Reforms*, Buckley attempts to counter his image as a nay-sayer by proposing specific remedies for the plight of schooling in America. None of his recommendations is particularly elitist, and all could conceivably help improve the lot of those disadvantaged persons for whom his opponents are perpetually claiming to speak.

The first of Buckley's proposals is put forth in his introduction. Here, he addresses himself to two recent demographic trends: the increase in population among the very old and the very young. One of the most vexing social problems which this nation faces (in the opinion of James A. Michener, *the* most serious challenge for the balance of this century) is providing care for the elderly. By increasing life expectancy, medical science has made it possible for us to enjoy more years of ill health than ever before.

But what, one might ask, does this have to do with the education of the young? Well, when one tallies up the expense of caring for the aged, "the only variable is in the cost of unskilled labor" (*FR*, 12). Specifically, what Buckley is suggesting is that the trustees of the nation's top ten private colleges announce that no freshman will be matriculated without first having devoted a year to public service. (Although more labor would be generated than the nursing homes could absorb, there are plenty of other—less pressing—jobs which need to be done.)

The virtues of this plan are several. First, since the initiative would come from the private sector, the state would not be conscripting people into philanthropic endeavors. Second, we would have found a cost-effective means of meeting urgent social needs. And finally, if education is understood as involving more than mere academic training, the young people participating in such a program would gain an educational advantage which many of our current undergraduates lack—a sense of moral responsibility.

In the main body of *Four Reforms,* its author devotes an entire chapter to what he calls "noncoerced education" in the nation's elementary and secondary schools. To bring about this noncoerced education, he proposes the following amendment to the constitution: *"No child shall be denied admission to a public school, by the United States or by an State, on account of race, creed, color, or national origin, notwithstanding any provision in the Constitution of the United States or of any State. Nor shall any relief authorized by any legislature for children attending nonpublic schools be denied by virtue of any provision in the Constitution of the United States or of any State"* (FR, 101).

The practical effect of such an amendment would be to prevent the courts from ordering busing or from prohibiting aid to private schools. From a formalistic standpoint, Buckley tends to favor those constitutional amendments which would limit judicial power and to oppose those which would expand that power. Ever since *Marbury* vs. *Madison* established the principle of judicial review, the courts—particularly the Supreme Court—have been the final arbiters of constitutional disputes. As a result, an activist judiciary (such as the Warren Court) has been able to make social policy rather than simply interpret the law. The mandating of busing and the outlawing of assistance to nonpublic schools are only two areas in which the courts have usurped what are essentially legislative prerogatives.[2]

The substantive advantage of this amendment would be to increase the freedom of choice which parents may exercise in determining where they will send their children to school. By making busing a constitutional right, the courts have institutionalized that remedy without sufficient regard to its *educational* effectiveness or its popular acceptance. When the schools become laboratories for social experimentation, they tend to lose sight of their primary objective. Also, it is difficult for a highly politicized school system to command the broad public support that it needs in order to function in a democratic society.

The argument for granting aid to private schools is both economic and philosophical. At the economic level, private schools educate children who would otherwise be in the public system. It is cheaper to allow such schools to survive by giving them some aid than to force them to close, and thus incur the expense of teaching all students in the public sector. In fact, one recent study suggests that a system of tax credits for parents of private school children would reduce the present cost of public schooling by encouraging even more students to transfer from public to private education.[3]

The philosophical case for public aid to private schools rests primarily on the value of pluralism (the more educational choices available to students today, the more richly diverse society will be tomorrow). Since the wealthy have always been able to send their children to private schools, any program (tax credits, academic vouchers,[4] etc.) which would extend this option to those with low and middle incomes is essentially populist and egalitarian in nature. Indeed, among the principal beneficiaries of such a program would be ghetto blacks who could more easily afford to attend the inner-city parochial schools to which they have recently fled in quest of an education superior to that available in the public system.[5]

From Things That Go Bump in the Night

In the fall of 1951, a recent Yale graduate named William F. Buckley, Jr. burst on the political scene with a controversial attack on his *alma mater*. Commenting on that attack, Max Eastman writes: "It was always a particular joy if some boy got up the nerve to throw an eraser or a piece of chalk when the teacher turned his back. Bill Buckley throws a whole handful right at the teacher and right while he is looking."[6] Subtitled *The Superstitions of "Academic Freedom,"* *God and Man at Yale*[7] raised practical and theoretical issues which are still being debated three decades later.

On the practical side, Buckley exposes the secularist and collectivist sympathies of several of Yale's more influential professors. It is somewhat anomalous, he argues, that Christian capitalists should pay to have their sons indoctrinated with values hostile to God and to the free market. The only possible explanation is that the university's alumni really do not know what is being taught in the classrooms that their contributions help to support. With the urgency of a latter-day Paul Revere (or Torquemada), Buckley sets out to expose the seamy truth.

Viewed from the perspective of the 1980s, the only thing about the furor surrounding *God and Man at Yale* which seems more dated than its author's outrage is that of his critics.[8] That the majority of professors in a "modern" university would smirk at the claims of Jesus Christ and Adam Smith is today almost a foregone conclusion (a classic dog-bites-man story). By objecting to Yale's ideological drift, Buckley may remind some of a moral majoritarian trying to stamp out smut. By denying the existence of such a drift, the university's "defenders" resemble nothing so much as cultural relativists asserting the redeeming social importance of a stag film.

At this late date, we are too far removed from the personalities and incidents which Buckley discusses to quibble over particulars. On the whole, his description of the theological and economic opinions prevalent at Yale seems more convincing than any of the attempts made to refute that description. Objections can be raised, however, to the way in which his argument is framed.

To begin with, one does not need to be an ardent collectivist to find the connection which Buckley proclaims between religion and economics to be a bit asymmetrical. Consider, for example, a particularly audacious passage in the foreword to *God and Man at Yale:* "I myself believe that the duel between Christianity and atheism is the most important in the world. I further believe that the struggle between individualism and collectivism is the same struggle reproduced on another level" (*GM,* xii–xiii). Although this formulation was actually supplied by Willmoore Kendall, it expresses a point of view which Buckley defends to this day.[9] That defense, however, consists of little more than an *ad hominem* attack on "Christian modernists" who believe "that the road to Christianity on earth lies through the Federal Government" (*H,* 425).

As a proponent of both Christianity and private enterprise, Buckley tilts his lance against irreligious socialists, but it is possible to imagine configurations of belief which do not conform to this neat dichotomy. What are we to do with a Christian advocate of the welfare state or with an atheistic supporter of the free market—with a Garry Wills or a Max Eastman? Such a dilemma may not be germane to the concrete situation discussed in *God and Man at Yale,* but it is surely pertinent to the philosophical issues which that book raises.

The fundamental question to which Buckley addresses himself is one of epistemology. Before we can begin to reform any particular university, we must have some concept of the ideal university; which is to say, we must define the nature of truth. Not surprisingly, the author of *God and Man at Yale* has fewer difficulties than most people in doing precisely that. In an essay on "The Aimlessness of American Education" (*R,* 98–108), he writes: "Schools ought not to be neutral. Schools should *not* proceed as though the wisdom of our fathers were too tentative to serve as an educational base. . . . Certain great truths have been apprehended. In the field of morality, all the basic truths have been apprehended; and we are going to teach these, and teach, and demonstrate, how it is that those who disregard them fall easily into the alien pitfalls of communism, or fascism, or liberalism" (*R,* 106).

If we are to inculcate in students a sense of values and a reverence for truth, we must not be afraid of practicing indoctrination, nor must we permit excessive heterodoxy. "[I]t does not make sense to suggest, as it everywhere is, that academic freedom should constrain a teaching institution to keep a teacher on even if he devotes himself to undermining the premises of the school at which he teaches, or the society in which he lives" (*R,* 104). Or, to put it another way: "Tolerance cannot be indiscriminate and equal with respect to the contents of expression, neither in word nor in deed; it cannot protect false words and wrong deeds. . . . Society cannot be indiscriminate . . . where freedom and happiness themselves are at stake: Here, certain things cannot be said, certain ideas cannot be expressed, certain policies cannot be proposed, certain behavior cannot be permitted."[10]

This latter statement comes not from any of Buckley's works, but from Herbert Marcuse's essay on "Repressive Tolerance." Although it would be simplistic to say that in the circular world of political ideology opposite extremes tend to merge, it is interesting to note the theoretical similarities between what critics on both the right and the left have to say about certain cherished liberal doctrines. In the area of higher education, for example, the myth of value neutrality is attacked with equal vigor and cogency by Buckley in *God and Man at Yale* and by Robert Paul Wolff in *The Ideal of the University.*

Just as Buckley asserts the existence of an implicit orthodoxy at Yale, so too does Wolff dismiss the absurdity of a free marketplace of ideas. "As a prescription for institutional behavior," Wolff writes, "the doctrine of value neutrality suffers from the worst disability which can afflict a norm: what it prescribes is not wrong; it is impossible."[11] Later he says: "By permitting all voices to be heard, the university systematically undermines all those doctrines [including Buckley's?] which claim exclusive possession of the truth and seek therefore to silence opposed voices. . . . For some strange reason, American intellectuals cannot perceive that their own commitment to free debate is also a substantive political act, no more neutral than the prohibition of dissent in religiously or politically authoritarian countries."[12]

The point which is being made by both the New Left and the Old Right is that a university, like any other institution, cannot act without at least tacitly acknowledging certain moral biases. In fact, the university not only harbors such biases while pretending not to, it also uses the illusion of impartiality to conceal its promulgation of values which its financial supporters would vigorously oppose. Since the Left generally benefits from this duplicity, Buckley is outraged by it. For the same reason, Wolff finds it a useful hypocrisy.[13]

As is the case with so many of Buckley's writings, *God and Man at Yale* is much more effective on the attack than on the defense. What is under attack here is the concept of academic freedom. The basic problem with that concept, Buckley argues, is that it depends on a blind faith in the epistemological optimism of such works as Milton's *Aereopagitica* and Mill's *Essay on Liberty*. Summarizing the thesis of these works, he writes: *"Let truth and error do battle in the arena of ideas. Truth will vanquish. Let the student and the citizen witness the struggle; let the struggle take place in their minds, and they will ally themselves with truth"* (*GM*, 156). To see that such a view is more a pious hope than a hard-headed assessment of reality, we need only remember that in Germany under Hitler, in Italy under Mussolini, and in Russia under Stalin, truth did not triumph.

When foolish optimism is thwarted too obviously and too often, it can degenerate into its opposite—hardened skepticism. Since so much of the world's evil is produced by those zealously seeking to enforce their personal vision of the good, would it not be safer to advance no orthodoxy and leave each man alone to cultivate his own intellectual garden? Unfortunately, as Wolff has pointed out, such value neutrality is a contradiction in terms, since neutrality is itself a value. To hold consistently to the tenets of axiological laissez faire, Buckley contends, one would have to support the right of a Joyce Kilmer aficionado to teach English at Yale—side by side with Cleanth Brooks and Robert Penn Warren.

If academic freedom is a snare and a delusion to be abominated by all right-thinking men, on what principle *should* the university constitute itself? For Buckley, the answer lies in replacing the marketplace of ideas with the literal marketplace. "In the last analysis," he writes, "academic freedom must mean the freedom of men and women to supervise the educational activities and aims of the schools they oversee and support (*GM*, 190).

Reflecting on this position a quarter-century after the publication of *God and Man at Yale*, its author cites a supporting statement by Irving Kristol: "Business men or corporations do not have any obligation to give money to institutions whose views or attitudes they disapprove of. It's absurd to insist otherwise—yet this absurdity is consistently set forth in the name of 'academic freedom'" (*H*, 439). In education, as in most other things, the consumer is proclaimed to be sovereign.

The problem with consumer sovereignty, however, is that it is no more adequate as an absolute philosophy than is academic freedom. When carried to its logical extreme, either position reduces itself to a practical absurdity. For legitimate reasons, there are some things which no consumer is allowed to purchase (such as the services of an arsonist or a hit man). Although it may be useful for certain analytical purposes to think of education as a consumer product, we must not assume that the customer is always right.

Of course, it might be objected that Buckley is not urging the Yale administration to hire arsonists or hit men (neither are the advocates of academic freedom urging it to hire Kilmerites); however, egregious abuses of consumer power do occur on the nation's campuses. We all know of the prominent alumnus who attempts to secure preferential academic treatment for a son or for a favorite athlete (the mere possibility of such interference is enough to intimidate some teachers). In our litigious age, even the poor can get in on the act. At many schools, public and private, craven administrators will regularly change a teacher's grades rather than run the risk of a student law suit. While I am certain that Buckley would deplore such practices, he must invoke some principle other than consumer sovereignty to do so.

The consumer model of education is inadequate not because ivory tower liberals should be allowed to force Irving Kristol's beleagured businessman into financing seditious professors, but because of the damage that model can do to the very concept of education. Clearly, consumers have their rights. But products also have their integrity. Theoretically, the consumer has sufficient power to work his will on the university; however, if he is a judicious man, he will exercise moderation and restraint in so doing. Otherwise, what he purchases from the academy can be called education only in the sense that what one purchases from a prostitute can be called romantic love.

Assuming the accuracy of his charges, Buckley is quite right to criticize Yale (or any other university) for being monolithically liberal. But the solution, it seems to me, is not so much to erect a conservative countermonolith as it is to provide advocates of diverse points of view with balanced access to the university (perhaps by giving academic credit for watching *Firing Line*).

In *God and Man at Yale*, we read of the wife of a prominent professor who suggested that the university offer a course in Communism "taught by a man who is neither pro-Communist nor anti-Communist" (*GM*, 176). Although Buckley scoffs at such a proposal, as well he should, perhaps he would consider a counterproposal: a course in Communism team-taught by Gus Hall and himself. After letting Gus ramble on for the entire semester, Buckley need only get up at the last class meeting, flash his impish grin, and say: "I rest my case."

Ironically, the illiberal behavior of student radicals during the sixties and early seventies caused many conservatives to discover the strategic value of tolerance. A good example of this is Buckley's own 1972 essay "Generals and Kids at Yale" (*EE*, 375–77). Here, he describes the successful efforts of shouters and hecklers to prevent General Westmoreland from speaking before the Yale students' Political Union. He then cites, with evident approval, Eugene Rostow's criticism of the student militants and of the university's failure to discipline them. The position which Buckley affirms is not that Westmoreland's right to speak derives from the objective truth of his message, but that such a right is vouchsafed by "the commitment of the university to *academic freedom*" (*EE*, 376; my italics).

Finally, this inchoate change in Buckley's position is made much more explicit in his 1977 essay "God and Man at Yale: Twenty-five Years Later": "In the ideal university all sides of any issue are presented as impartially and as forcefully as possible. . . . In a world governed by compromise, in which opportunism can be virtuous—such a world as our own—I am obliged to confess: I probably would settle for such an arrangement. A truly balanced curriculum, in which as much time, by professors as talented as their counterparts, in courses as critical as the others, were given to demonstrating the cogency of the arguments for God and man" (*H*, 444–45).

I am reminded of an incident which took place during Eugene McCarthy's 1976 campaign for president. Mistaking him for the earlier Senator McCarthy, a questioner asked "Clean Gene" why he was no longer so obsessed with Communism. To which the candidate replied: "I guess we've all mellowed over the years."

Chapter Nine

Soulcraft

Despite the efforts of our deistic forefathers to erect a wall between religious and civil authority, American churchmen have rarely been content simply to render unto God while ignoring Caesar. Indeed, the meddling of religion in politics is as American as Prohibition and the Underground Railroad. The process, however, has generally not worked the other way around. The protestations of Jerry Falwell and Bob Jones to the contrary notwithstanding, government usually has been reluctant to interfere with the free exercise of religion. Instead, what has emerged in recent years is an independent critique of the behavior of churches toward the political order and a fresh examination of ecclesiastical polity itself.

As a committed Christian and political activist, Bill Buckley has involved himself in controversies both within and between church and world. For a Roman Catholic of pre–Vatican II vintage, such controversies were particularly acute during the 1960s and 70s. In 1960, a church which previously had sought to compensate for its theocratic reputation by remaining outside national politics had gained new visibility with the election of a Catholic president. (Ironically, within a decade, opposition to the war which that president did so much to escalate would bring a growing number of priests and nuns into the political arena.) At the same time, the Second Vatican Council was radically altering centuries of liturgical tradition. We were entering an era in which the mere act of eating fish on Friday caused one to appear more Catholic than the Pope.

Rendering Unto Caesar

In 1961, Pope John XXIII issued an encyclical on social justice entitled *Mater et Magistra.* Received warmly by Catholic liberals, this document proved something of an embarrassment to those who wished to remain loyal to the Church while maintaining a conservative political ideology. Characteristically, *National Review* pulled no punches in deploring what it regarded as the pontiff's misplaced rhetorical emphases. Indeed, an editorial paragraph devoted to the encyclical contains the provocative conclusion: "Whatever its final effect, . . . [*Mater et Magistra*] must strike many as a venture in triviality coming at this particular time in history." And, two weeks later, the journal crystallized its position with the following observation: "Going the rounds in conservative Catholic circles: 'Mater, si; Magistra, no.'"[1] As one might expect, when these comments became known among left-wing Catholics, the holy water really hit the fan.

Leading the opposition was the Jesuit-edited weekly *America;* however, the syndicated columnists who appear in diocesan newspapers were not far behind. The Reverend William J. Smith, for example, weighed in with the following: "A venture in triviality! Where will one find so insulting, so stupid a statement as that? . . . When a spiritual intellectual giant of the stature of Pope John XXIII is ridiculed by a hypercritical pigmy, the shout of protest should be loud and lasting. . . . This is the kind of stuff from which seedling schisms sprout."[2] Mr. Donald Mcdonald was equally acerbic: "If any Catholic is really uncertain concerning the comparative qualifications of Pope John on the one hand and William Buckley on the other to speak out on the great social problems of our age, no argument from me is likely to have much effect. . . . True conservatives must stand aghast at this latest display of anti-intellectual temper tantrums by the men at *National Review*."[3]

In an effort to get the editor of *America,* Father Thurston Davis, to call off his attack dogs, Buckley wrote a lengthy and sensible epistle to the Jesuit magazine. Not only did Father Davis refuse to publish Buckley's letter, but he also refused to accept any further advertising from *National Review.* (Five years earlier, he had blacklisted anyone whose name appeared on the *NR* masthead, even to the point of returning previously accepted articles by Russell Kirk and Erik von Kuehnelt-Leddihn.) In the name of liberal Christianity, *America* and its henchmen were conducting a Holy Inquisition against a secular journal for having the temerity to criticize the purely political insights of the Pope.

Hoping somehow to moderate this factional strife, Donald Thorman, the managing editor of Notre Dame's unofficial magazine *Ave Maria,* called upon Catholic liberals and conservatives alike to put an end to their "sometimes unhealthy, often unchristian—and totally unnecessary—internecine feud." "Is it out of the question," he wondered, "to hope that quiet meetings between members of both camps might be held to work out Christian ground rules for debate and to decide on a basic, minimal program for a united fight against Communism and for the promotion of justice and charity in our society?"[4] In response to Mr. Thorman's plea, Buckley contributed to *Ave Maria* an essay which was later published in *Rumbles Left and Right* under the title "Catholic Liberals, Catholic Conservatives, and the Requirements of Unity."

This essay begins by suggesting that the best that mediators like Thorman should hope for in terms of "a basic, minimal program" around which Catholic liberals and conservatives can unite would be a bipartisan strategy for resisting Communism. This is not because either camp is indifferent to the imperatives of justice and charity at home, but because their ideas about how to achieve those goals are so much at odds as to be functionally irreconcilable. The bulk of the essay, then, is devoted to a discussion of anti-Communism. Unfortunately, even here, Buckley seems less interested in establishing common ground than in pointing out the fallacies of liberal thought.

With the best intentions in the world, many pious individuals believe that virtue must ultimately triumph because of its inherent superiority to vice. Thus, if America wishes to prevail against Communism, it should strive to achieve social justice at home. In response to this notion, Buckley writes: "[I]t is theologically wrong, historically naive, and strategically suicidal to assume that the forces of Communism, like those of the devil, are routed by personal or even corporate acts of justice and love. Our fight against Communism is not to be understood merely as a fight against sin. . . . [T]he [salient] distinction is not between 'just' and 'unjust' acts in relation to fighting Communism, but between relevant and irrelevant means of fighting Communism" (*R*, 112–13).

Always alert for an historical analogy, Buckley recalls Abraham Lincoln's writing to Horace Greeley during the depths of the Civil War that he was more intent on preserving the union than on freeing the slaves. The point was that if the union were lost, so too would be the goal of emancipation. With the preservation of the union, however, "civilized discourse would resume, and men with black faces would in due course become free" (*R*, 115). After making his ideological points, Buckley held out an olive branch by inviting Father Davis to lunch to discuss their mutual differences. Rather than accept the luncheon invitation, Davis launched a new attack on Buckley—this time accusing him of anticlericalism!

The entire *Mater et Magistra* controversy was a kind of inverted, Kafkaesque farce in which the "liberals" advocated ecclesiastical authoritarianism in order to impose a political orthodoxy on independent-minded conservatives. "For a heady moment," Garry Wills writes, "the victims of heresy hunts . . . became heresy hunters themselves—as, they say, beaten children grow up to be childbeaters."[5] Indeed, "this was such a delightful game that even non-Catholics wanted to get in on it. Gore Vidal, who would write the introduction to a 1977 book calling Christ a fraud, professed shock on 'The Tonight Show' that Buckley would defy the Vicar of that Fraud."[6] As Murray Kempton noted: "Many of those who are in the field against Mr. Buckley would never think to bow [their] heads to the Cross except when it is withdrawn from him."[7]

If the issues treated in *Mater et Magistra* were ones about which Catholics were bitterly divided, the question of abortion clearly was not. Up through the late sixties, the vast majority of Roman Catholics (and, indeed, Americans in general) were convinced that abortion was so wrong that—except in very special circumstances—it should be proscribed by law. This consensus was only beginning to dissipate when, in January 1973, the Supreme Court handed down its historic decision in the case of *Roe* v. *Wade*. Essentially, this decision held that laws which had existed since the founding of our nation were in violation of the Fourteenth Amendment (a fact which had escaped the notice of the men who framed and ratified that amendment).

In response to those who might be tempted to write off his opposition to abortion as the knee-jerk reaction of a right-wing Catholic, Buckley notes:

It is true that the anti-abortion movement is perceived as a substantially Catholic movement, but it is by no means nourished by exclusively Catholic theology. Jews and Protestants in significant numbers are opposed to abortion for religious reasons. Anyway, religion nowhere tells them thou shalt not kill a fetus; religion tells them simply thou shalt not kill a human being. It is scientific evidence, not religious evidence, that leads them to believe, as so many doctors and scientists are coming to believe, that a fetus is in every crucial respect except one a human being, entitled, therefore, to be treated as one would a day-old baby. (*H*, 282)

(As Buckley's lucid exposition makes clear, one of the ironic aspects of the abortion controversy is that it unites religion and science against superstition and ideology. When Congress held hearings to try to determine when human life begins, that effort was opposed by the proabortion crowd on the grounds that it might compromise a woman's right to control her own body. Thus, did today's feminists uphold the anti-intellectual tradition of Dayton, Tennessee.)

Buckley is wise not to articulate his antiabortion position in the "profamily" rhetoric of the New Right. (To the extent that the cause of the unborn has come to be associated in the public mind with the likes of Phyllis Schlafly and Jesse Helms, the average American probably thinks of it as having something to do with the Panama Canal and busing.) Instead, he once again calls up the specter of Abraham Lincoln to suggest that conservatives are really less illiberal than their brethren on the left. The *Roe* v. *Wade* decision, he argues, is the Dred Scott decision of the twentieth century. If a civil war could be fought over the humanity of blacks, is it any wonder that the humanity of the fetus has generated such an intense political debate?

Perhaps Buckley's most original contribution to the dialogue over abortion was to inject a note of levity into the proceedings. But then, it is only right that an issue which has been discussed with saccharine piety, philosophical rigor, and ideological hysteria finally be subjected to the tonic of wit. The victim of that wit is not the unwed mother herself, but that self-appointed arbiter of public morality—the American Civil Liberties Union.

It seems that in 1977 the New Orleans chapter of the Civil Liberties Union raised funds for its good deeds by auctioning off a whole range of professional services donated by supporters of the organization. Among those services was one free abortion. Since the Supreme Court, an unpredictable bunch if there ever was one, had recently ruled that states were not constitutionally required to pick up the tab for elective abortions, it seemed only right that compassionate private sector types take up the slack. Otherwise, many feared that "from now on only Doris Duke can get an abortion; [and that] everyone else will need to go to the nearest Snidely J. Whiplash in a grimy basement, or—as in the movie *The Other Side of Midnight*—to a clothes-hanger" (*H,* 283). Imagine, then, the chagrin of all concerned when the free scrape brought $30 on the open market.

If the free-market value of a New Orleans abortion is only $30, then we need not stay up nights worrying about those who cannot afford one: "Just about everybody can afford $30. And since you can't have an abortion more often than once every couple of months, you can keep a special piggy bank for the purpose" (*H*, 284). The ACLU would thus be free to auction off more valuable services. Such as a free defense for rape. "If they maneuver the very best lawyer in New Orleans into making that contribution, then the successful bidder might figure he has in effect bought himself one free rape. In the land of noblesse oblige, the same bidder might also buy the free abortion voucher—which he could then stuff down the dress of the girl" (*H*, 284–85). If such a Swiftian proposal might strike some as a trifle immodest, it may simply be that the very topic of abortion nurtures one's sense of absurdity. After all, it is the only surgical procedure that is judged a success if the patient dies.

A Piece of the Rock

The trials and tribulations of the post–Vatican II Catholic Church have received extensive coverage in the secular press. In one of its periodic contributions to that coverage, *Time* quotes an "elderly woman parishoner of St. Thomas Aquinas Church, Ames, Iowa" as saying: "I hope I die soon so that I can die a Catholic." Bill Buckley begins one of *his* periodic essays on the agonies of Catholicism by declaring this epigram to be both an expression of considerable sentiment within the Church and philosophically perplexing: "Rather like the story of the man whose doctor informs him that he has terminal cancer, and asks what he proposes to do. The patient reflects for a moment, and then says he will join the Communist Party. 'Better one of them should go than one of us'" (*H*, 285).

Buckley's own stance toward Mother Church may well be described as a conflict of sentiment and philosophy. Although he is appalled by the theological and liturgical trends of recent years, he is unwilling to follow the lead of those who, like French Archbishop Marcel Le Febvre, seek to uphold Catholic tradition by defying the institutional church. Instead, he functions as a loyal opposition—remaining in his pew as a sort of ecclesiastical gadfly.

Probably the most egregious corruption of Catholic ritual to come out of Vatican II was the end of the Latin Mass. For Buckley and countless others, this ancient liturgy had produced "something akin to that synesthesia which nowadays most spiritually restless folk find it necessary to discover in drugs or from a guru in mysterious India" (*JE*, 288). Not only was the language of the Mass translated into the vernacular, but the entire service was redesigned so as to replace a transcendent experience with a merely communal one. Consider, for example, the following description of a Mass celebrated in the gymnasium of a Catholic high school: "A poster directly behind the altar was of an enormous catsup bottle and the message, 'If you're a plump tomato, Hunts has an opening for you.' On either side of the altar were 'box art' figures, about five feet high, of Martin Luther King, Bob Dylan, John Lennon, the Mahirishi what's his name, Gandhi, Thurgood Marshall. Above the altar was suspended a large mobile made of pieces of broken glass and tin cans and a sign asking 'What's your story, people?'" (GL, 289).

The rationale behind the greening of Christianity is that religion must be relevant to the modern world; in the words of Paul Seabury, it must be "trendier than thou."[8] However, such a strategy all too often succeeds only in alienating the old guard while making minimal impact upon the secular world. Moreover, the new latitudinarianism can be just as rigid and uncharitable as the old triumphalism. There is perhaps as much poignance as humor to Sir Arnold Lunn's observation that if preserving one Latin Mass each Sunday in the larger churches would serve only the educated few, "surely Mother Church in all her charity can find a place even for the educated few" (JE, 290).

It should be pointed out that Buckley is no mindless Tridentine bead-knocker, but a thoughtful critic of his church. In endorsing a more relaxed policy toward contraception, divorce, and clerical celibacy,[9] he urges the Roman Communion to change more than it has in the area of sexual morality. The issue is not whether one is for or against change, but what sort of change one advocates. By being more liberal than Paul VI in some matters and more conservative in others, Buckley is probably close to the mainstream of American Catholicism. As many have concluded, more in sorrow than in condemnation, the late pontiff gave up what he should have held on to and held on to what he should have given up.

Of course, with the Roman Church, it is at least possible to know what is being given up and what is being held on to. Adherents to the Anglican faith are not always so sure. As Auberon Waugh once pointed out: "In England we have a curious institution called the Church of England. . . . Its strength has always lain in the fact that on any moral or political issue it can produce such a wide divergence of opinion that nobody—from the Pope to Mao Tse Tung—can say with any confidence that he is not an Anglican. Its weaknesses are that nobody pays much attention to it and very few people attend its functions" (EE, 459). Indeed, given the comprehensiveness of the Anglican Communion, about the only issues which could have created dissension within its ranks were the ordination of women and revision of The Book of Common

Prayer. With an unerring death wish, church activists undertook both reforms in the 1970s.

Since prayer book revision was a protracted activity which took well over a decade to consummate, defenders of the old rite—both Anglican and non-Anglican—had ample opportunity to make their case. A Roman Catholic who was all too familiar with the fruits of reform, Buckley added his voice to the chorus of protest. Residing somewhere on that great spectrum between the Bishop of Rome and Chairman Mao, he could even claim to be an Anglican.

If it could be plausibly argued that translating the Latin Mass into modern English would enhance comprehension, it is hard to say the same about *The Book of Common Prayer.* A volume which is no more difficult to understand than the King James Bible and is considerably less demanding than the plays of Shakespeare is obviously accessible to more than just the educated few. In fact, if the modern translation of the Lord's Prayer is any indication, liturgical revision may actually have helped to reduce intelligibility. What can one say, for example, about replacing "Lead us not into temptation" with "Do not bring us to the time of trial"? Commenting on this travesty, Buckley writes: "I know, because every sense in my body informs me, and every misinclination of my mind, what is temptation, from which we seek deliverance. But *'the time of trial'*? That sounds like the Supreme Court is in session" (*H,* 289).[10]

No reasonable person could deny the need for change, even in seemingly timeless religious practices. However, gratuitous or harmful change ought to be opposed. What is most distressing is that at the root of many of the modernist trends in Christianity is a secularizing impulse. Historically, whenever such an impulse prevails, people tend to seek more exotic means of cultivating their religious sensibilities. (The transcendentalist movement in mid-nineteenth-century New England was more a reaction against Unitarian rationalism than against Puritan theocracy. By the same token, today's Moonies and Hare Krishnas seem to be rebelling against a culture in which religion has come to mean little more than a Sunday morning social hour.)

Always alert to entrepreneurial possibilities, Buckley speculates that if he were ever broke, he would "repair to India [and] haul up a guru's flag." There, he would minister to the Beatles, Mia Farrow, and any other celebrity pilgrim by coming up with lines like the following: "Put on, therefore, as the elect of God, holy and beloved, bowels of mercies, kindness, humbleness of mind, meekness, long-suffering; forbearing one another, and forgiving one another, if any man have a quarrel against any; even as ———— forgave you, so also do ye. And above all these things put on charity, which is the bond of perfectness. And let the peace of God rule in your hearts, to the which also ye are called in one body; and be thankful" *(GL, 301)*.

"The truly extraordinary feature of our time," Buckley observes, "isn't the faithlessness of the Western people; it is their utter, total ignorance of the Christian religion. They travel to Rishikesh to listen to pallid seventh-hand imitations of thoughts and words they never knew existed. They will go anywhere to experience spirituality—except next door" *(GL, 301-2)*. Of course, if what is going on next door is a neo-modernist encounter group posing as Christianity, it is questionable whether the ensuing experience could properly be labeled as spirituality. Still, the Christian faith maintains some advantages over upstart creeds. When asked by a disciple what he might do to start a new religion, Voltaire recommended: "begin by getting yourself killed. Then rise again on the third day" *(GL, 302)*.

Although he is committed to both Christianity and conservatism, Buckley is neither a Catholic theocrat nor a moral majoritarian. (Indeed, in the *Mater et Magistra* controversy he was arguing for the toleration of political pluralism within the Catholic Church, while his "liberal" attackers came off like Falwells of the Left seeking to impose a religious party line.) Nevertheless, he sees religion and politics as being fundamentally related—at a theoretical if not an operational level.[11] Any political philosophy which is more than simply a partisan game plan must spring from a metaphysical—which is to say, a religious—matrix. In Buckley's case, that matrix is a fairly traditional form of Catholic piety. (Like George F. Will, he regards statecraft as essentially soulcraft.) Asked by *Playboy* whether "most dogmas, theological as well as ideological, [do not] crumble sooner or later," he replied: "Most, but not all." How could he be so sure, *Playboy* wondered. Because, Buckley proclaimed, "I know that my Redeemer liveth" *(I, 64)*.

Chapter Ten
Strictly Personal

It has become rather commonplace for opponents who have gotten to know William Buckley to comment on the dichotomy between his public and his private personalities. One such individual, who is identified only as a "liberal Catholic editor," has said: "It's as though he's in uniform while in public and is willing, like a soldier, to do whatever has to be done. Then he takes off the uniform and you have the friendly guy who'll grant you points, merry and relaxed, and who would never dream of hurting someone's feelings."[1] Not surprisingly, some of Buckley's warmest and most engaging essays have been written when their author was at parade rest.

The Fingernail of a Saint

If the struggle against Communism was the single most galvanizing force for the post–World War II Right, then the contemporary conservative movement owes its very existence to former leftists who—like Saul on the Road to Damascus—shifted loyalties from one extreme commitment to another. (Indeed, if we follow the McCarthyite practice of holding a man's past allegiances against him, the greatest nest of subversives to be found in America during the fifties may have been the editorial board of *National Review.*) Among those making the political pilgrimage from left to right were such luminaries as Max Eastman, James Burnham, and John Dos Passos. None of their conversions, however, had nearly so dramatic an impact on American life as that of a brilliant, tormented Soviet agent named Whittaker Chambers.

Probably no single act did greater damage to the liberal hegemony of the New Deal–Fair Deal years than Chambers's exposure of Alger Hiss. That such a quintessentially establishment figure as Hiss could have been a Communist spy was bad enough, but the eagerness of high government officials—including President Truman and Secretary of State Acheson—to rush to his defense suggested to many that we were being governed by knaves and fools. The Hiss case also made Richard Nixon a national figure and helped give Joe McCarthy the issue which he so egregiously exploited. In addition, it provided conservatives with a cause more popular than the elimination of Social Security or the canonization of Edmund Burke.

Bill Buckley first met Whittaker Chambers in 1954, several years after the Hiss case and just prior to the founding of *National Review*. Although he was impressed with *McCarthy and His Enemies*, judging it to be a much better defense than the senator deserved, Chambers refused to squander his prestige as an anti-Communist by writing a blurb for the book. Quite perceptively, he noted that *"for the Right to tie itself in any way to Senator McCarthy is suicide. Even if he were not what, poor man, he has become, he can't lead anybody because he can't think"* (R, 147).[2] Later, when Buckley was courting him for the masthead of *National Review*, Chambers expressed caution about joining any enterprise which might support McCarthy and be less than enthusiastic about Eisenhower and Nixon.

Tired cliché though it may be, the label "man of contradictions" clearly fits Whittaker Chambers. Unlike so many who moved from the left to the right, he sought to wage a moderate and pragmatic war against Communism rather than launch an eye-gouging witch hunt. Indeed, his devotion to civil liberties was such that he even defended Alger Hiss's right to travel abroad when Hiss was denied a passport. A prophet who viewed the world with apocalyptic gloom, he was nevertheless "a highly amusing and easily amused man. . . . He was not merely a man of wit, but also a man of humor, and even a man of fun" (R, 157).

Although he did align himself with *National Review* for awhile, Chambers was never comfortable as a schematic conservative. Ever the loner, he wrote to Buckley: *"You . . . stand within, or at any rate are elaborating, a political orthodoxy. I stand within no political orthodoxy. . . . I am at heart a counter-revolutionist"* (R, 159). Having rejected one dogmatic world view, he was not eager to embrace another. Indeed, one senses that the purity of his message would have been attenuated had he been too easily pigeonholed as a right-wing theoretician. He was quite simply what the title of his autobiography proclaimed him to be—a "Witness." After reading that autobiography, André Malraux wrote to Chambers: "You have not come back from hell with empty hands" (R, 159).

In one of his few sensible statements, Charles Lam Markmann characterizes Chambers as an American analogue to Malraux: "the totally engaged intellectual."[3] The accuracy of this observation is suggested by Chambers's attempt to explain his radical past to Buckley. *"I came to communism,"* he writes, *"above all under the influence of the* Narodniki . . . *'those who went with bomb or revolver against this or that individual monster.' Unlike most Western Communists, who became Communists under the influence of the Social Democrats, I remained under the influence of the Narodniki long after I became a Marxist. In fact, I never threw it off. I never have. It has simply blended with that strain of the Christian tradition to which it is akin"* (R, 149). So committed was Chambers that, upon learning of his conversion, a former comrade declared: *"I simply cannot believe that Whittaker Chambers has broken, I could believe it of anybody else, but not of him"* (R, 149).

The victim of a series of heart attacks, Chambers died in 1961. Both the character of the man and what he stood for continue to live, however, in the influence which he exerted on Bill Buckley. Although tracing the origins of any man's thought and personality is a highly speculative undertaking, one cannot help but believe that his association with Chambers helped to nourish Buckley's own reservoirs of wit and tenderness. If the dogmatic irascibility of Willmoore Kendall is evident in Buckley's first two books, that quality seems to have been lightened and humanized in the writings which came after he knew Chambers. Nowhere is this more evident than in his moving tribute to his friend.

"The Last Years of Whittaker Chambers" begins with Buckley's waiting under Renoir's "Girl with the Watering Can" at the National Gallery in Washington for what turns out to be his last encounter with Chambers. From there, they attend the very private wedding of Chambers's son John. Having done penance for his earlier treason and raised his children, Whittaker Chambers felt free to lay down the burden that was his life. "He died a month later, on July 9, 1961. Free at last" (R, 146).

Moving backward through the years of their friendship, Buckley intersperses his own description and commentary with generous excerpts from Chambers's letters. At the end, we see a man of such deep humility and intellectual curiosity that he spent the final months of his life studying science at a nearby college, while taking Latin, Greek, and advanced French composition for fun. There, a coed who helped him dissect the cadavers of frogs asked one of the most important intellectuals of our time what he thought of *Itsy Bitsy Teenie Weenie Yellow Polka Dot Bikini*. Upon ascertaining that the phenomenon in question was a popular song, the Witness testified to its being indisputably his favorite piece of music.

On a more somber note, he described our present malaise as follows:

It is idle to talk about preventing the wreck of Western civilization. It is already a wreck from within. That is why we can hope to do little more now than snatch a fingernail of a

*saint from the rack or a handful of ashes from the faggots, and bury them in a flowerpot
against the day, ages hence, when a few men begin again to dare to believe that there was
once something else, that something else is thinkable, and need some evidence of what it
was, and the fortifying knowledge that there were those who, at the great nightfall, took
loving thought to preserve the tokens of hope and truth* (R, 148).

Not Wisely But Too Well

On October 1, 1976, a young woman was accosted on a San Diego
street by a man who dragged her to his car, demanding that she hand over
the money in her purse. When she resisted, he stabbed her with a six-inch
knife, just missing her vital organs. The woman managed to kick her feet
through the windshield of the car, lunge against the wheel, and force the
vehicle to lurch to the side of the road. Somehow, she was able to open the
door and roll out on to the sidewalk in the presence of half-a-dozen
witnesses. Her attacker was apprehended a few weeks later when he placed
a desperation phone call to the offices of *National Review*. Although his
good friend Bill Buckley was not in at the time, Buckley promptly notified
the FBI when he was informed of the call.

The man in question was Edgar H. Smith, Jr., a convicted murderer
who had spent more time on death row than any other prisoner in
American history. He had come to William Buckley's attention in the
early 1960s when an article in a New Jersey newspaper reporting on a day
in the life of death-row inmate Edgar Smith mentioned that he used to
read *National Review* but no longer did so because the chaplain whose copy
he used to borrow had been transferred. Buckley then wrote to Smith to
ask if he would like to receive a complimentary subscription to *NR*.
Subsequently, Buckley developed an interest in the Smith case, became
convinced of the man's innocence, and devoted considerable time and
money to the battle to save Smith from the electric chair.

Edgar Smith had been convicted of the 1957 murder of a flirtatious
adolescent named Victoria Zielinski. According to the government's case,
Smith had picked up Miss Zielinski, driven her to a nearby sandpit, and
attempted to seduce her. When she resisted and ran away, he is supposed
to have chased her through the sandpit with a baseball bat, hit her with the
bat, and brought her back to the pit, where he proceeded to splatter her
brains with a heavy boulder. After investigating the case with the zeal of a
Perry Mason, Buckley concluded that it would have been nearly impossible for Smith to have committed the murder in the time and under the
circumstances alleged by the prosecution. Moreover, the coroner's report

established the time of instantaneous death as several hours after Smith had returned from the scene of the murder.

Buckley's involvement in the Smith case suggests that he possesses greater compassion for the underdog and greater concern for the rights of criminal defendants than one might imagine from his more general pronouncements. The principal irony of this case was that professed conservatives like Buckley and Smith were forced to appeal to the judiciary on procedural grounds established by the liberal Warren Court. Indeed, the most damaging evidence against Smith would have been ruled inadmissible had the decision in the case of *Mapp* v. *Ohio* (a particular *bête noire* of the right) been ruled retroactively applicable. Moreover, on one crucial appeal, the only Supreme Court justice to see things Smith's way was William O. Douglas. About which Smith wrote to Buckley: "Bless his liberal heart!!" (*JE,* 162).

After spending fourteen years on death row and twice coming within hours of execution, Edgar Smith finally convinced a judge that he had been unfairly tried. Rather than retry him for first-degree murder, the state of New Jersey persuaded Smith to plead guilty to second-degree murder in exchange for immediate release. Swallowing his pride, he copped the plea and left the Trenton State Prison for Bill Buckley's waiting car. The judge who ordered his release was certain that Edgar Smith had indeed killed Victoria Zielinski. However, he was just as certain that in his years on death row Smith had become a totally rehabilitated man. A member of Mensa, author of two best-selling books, and friend of William Buckley, he posed no realistic threat to society. Less than five years later, the friends and advocates of Edgar Smith were proved tragically wrong.

Although Buckley's defense of Smith was based on a sincere and reasonable belief in the man's innocence, the improbable friendship between a cultivated right-wing polemicist and a self-educated prisoner is somewhat more difficult to explain. Clearly, the phenomenon of the inmate-writer exercises a fascination over a certain segment of the American intelligentsia. While liberals are willing to lavish praise on such social misfits as Eldridge Cleaver, Caryl Chessman, and Jack Henry Abbott, Buckley chose to befriend a Catholic conservative whose prose style possessed an almost Victorian elegance. Whether Smith was hopelessly violent from the very beginning or whether he was irredeemably brutalized by the prison system is something we may never know. In any event, despite the inconsistencies in the prosecution's case against him, he now freely admits to having murdered Victoria Zielinski and, thus, to having deceived many good and intelligent people.

To his credit, Buckley does not apologize for his behavior in the Smith case. Edgar Smith was freed because a court had overturned his conviction and because a judge believed him to be rehabilitated, not because Bill Buckley exercises undue influence over the American judicial system. Mark Twain once observed that a cat who has sat on a hot stove will never do so again. Nor will he sit on a cold stove either. Not only must we learn from experience, but we should also be on guard against learning the wrong lesson. "There will be guilty people freed this year and every year," Buckley writes. "But for those who believe that the case of Edgar Smith warrants a vow to accept the ruling of a court as always definitive, it is only necessary to remind ourselves that, this year and every year, an innocent man will be convicted. Edgar Smith has done enough damage in his lifetime without underwriting the doctrine that the verdict of a court is infallible" (*H*, 397). What is also sadly fallible is one's faith in the redemption of any given individual. At worst, William Buckley loved not wisely but too well.

Tributes

The year 1964 was a crucial one for American conservatism. From 1940 through 1960, the Republican Party had been controlled by Eastern-seaboard moderates who managed to secure the presidential nomination for such middle-of-the-road types as Wendell Willkie, Thomas E. Dewey, Dwight Eisenhower, and Richard Nixon. Liberal Democrat John F. Kennedy had just been succeeded in the White House by the equally liberal Lyndon Johnson, and the most prominent Republican contender appeared to be that ultimate establishmentarian Nelson Rockefeller. It was at that dispirited moment that there arose in the West a right-wing savior named Barry Goldwater.

Goldwater's rugged western independence was combined with a personal sense of *noblesse oblige*,[4] which stressed voluntary benevolence and distrusted government interference in the private sector. After paying homage to the spirit of the Old Frontier, as opposed to the New one, Goldwater told Bill Buckley: "That was a spiritual energy that came out of the loins of the people. It didn't come out of Washington. And it never will. Washington's principal responsibility is to get out of the way of the creative impulses of the people" (*R*, 26). Unfortunately for the conservative movement, the American people were not ready for such a philosophy in 1964. (Elsewhere, Buckley has hypothesized that the electorate was *too conservative* to want a third president in little over a year.) Nevertheless, the

Goldwater wing gained such prominence within the Republican Party that not even Johnson's landslide victory could persuade the GOP to return to the "me-too" politics it had pursued in previous years.

In Buckley's opinion, Goldwater failed in his presidential bid not because he was behind the times, but because he was ahead of them. His principal service to the nation, then, was as a prophet crying in the wilderness. And like most prophets, he was calling the people back to an earlier covenant. He was, in short, a reeducator. When that political re-education is complete," Buckley wrote in 1963,"—perhaps during Goldwater's lifetime—a man such as he, with a program such as his, could lead the country" (*R*, 30–31). Such a man emerged as a national political figure because of his articulate support of the doomed Goldwater crusade. Had there been no Barry Goldwater, there would have been no Ronald Reagan.

When Reagan went on television in 1964 to preach the gospel according to Barry, the response was nearly $5 million in dollar-bill contributions and immediate talk about Reagan's own political potential. What few people realize is that that speech came very close to not being broadcast. An hour before it was to be shown statewide in California, word came from the Goldwater headquarters to hold off because of rumors that the speech was "too extreme." However, Reagan was able to get in touch with the candidate himself and assure him that there wasn't a "kooky line" in the speech (*JF*, 84–85). Had Reagan gotten Goldwater's answering service, the course of history might have been changed, forcing pundits of the 1980s to discourse on the legislative tribulations of President Jesse Helms.

After being elected Governor of California in 1966, Reagan became the most prominent conservative politician in America and an immediate presidential contender. In "A Relaxing View of Ronald Reagan," Bill Buckley gives his own impressions of the man and politician. Even though the subject of this essay would not enter the White House until 1981, what Buckley said of him in 1967 seems less dated than prescient. The qualities which would alternately baffle and charm a nation a decade-and-a-half later were evident early in Ronald Reagan's political career.

Shortly after his inauguration as governor, the fiscally conservative Reagan submitted the largest budget in the history of California. When this anomaly was cited, he defended himself by blaming conditions on the ineptitude of the previous administration. Although such an alibi has some validity, pointing as it does to the institutional inertia of government, it can lead to infinite regress. No doubt, George Washington blamed his problems on the mess left him by George III. Typically, liberals found Reagan too conservative, while Birchers thought him too liberal. For those who had no ideological ax to grind, he came off as surprisingly affable and moderate.

Much of Buckley's essay is devoted to showing Reagan as a man of mordant wit—a sort of conservative John F. Kennedy. And some of his one-liners are indeed eminently quotable. For example, when Buckley once remarked of a controversial public figure that he had the "face of a bank teller," Reagan replied: "Bank teller, hell, he has the face of the neighborhood child molester" (*JE*, 83). The governor is also depicted as a physically resourceful, take-charge guy. On one occasion, he inched his way along a narrow window ledge two stories above the ground to get into the locked equipment room of an auditorium where he was to speak. What Buckley fails to mention, what he may not realize, is that this particular maneuver comes from one of the early scenes of the much-maligned *Bedtime for Bonzo*. For Reagan, as for so many others in politics, life imitates art.

It should not be assumed that Bill Buckley writes admiringly only of co-ideologists. Perhaps because he is not temperamentally a conservative, he is known to have enjoyed the company of such left-leaning figures as John Kenneth Galbraith, Norman Mailer, Steve Allen, Murray Kempton, and the late Allard Lowenstein. Thus, it is not surprising that one of his most amusing and moving character sketches is an appreciation of the dying Hubert Horatio Humphrey.

From the time that his advocacy of civil rights split the 1948 Democratic Convention until his death three decades later, Humphrey was such a visible and vocal national presence that millions of Americans found it difficult to imagine the country without him. He was a resolutely partisan man who fought energetically for liberal social causes, only to find himself a pariah to the Left because of his loyal defense of Lyndon Johnson's tragically flawed Vietnam policies. At the end, however, the happy warrior miraculously transcended politics. Republicans and Democrats, liberals and conservatives, saw only his personal warmth, his irrepressible good nature, and a physical courage which reduced the most powerful men in America to tears.

Buckley's essay is entitled "A Tory's Tribute to Hubert Horatio Humphrey," and, as such, does not seek to minimize the political differences between author and subject. (Indeed, Buckley states those differences so energetically that the *New York Times Magazine* refused to run the piece on the grounds that it was "too savage" a treatment of a dying man.

Humphrey, however, enjoyed it when it was printed in *National Review* and had his assistant acknowledge that fact to Buckley—a courtesy which the senator's diminished energy prevented him from performing himself.) And yet, delineating those differences somehow misses the point. "[H]ow futile is the exercise [of criticism]," Buckley writes, "when we are engaged, in fact, in trying to console ourselves against the inconsolable reality, which is that this preposterous man, this man of majestic intellectual imprecision, this demagogue of transcendent gall, may not be with us forever. What is it about him that causes this sadness to well up, even in those Tories he has sought so diligently to exile?" (*H,* 172).

Although he confesses to not having the answer to this question, Buckley does describe a personal experience which tells us much about the essential Humphrey. The scene was the forward compartment of a Pan Am 727. There were only eight or ten passengers "but when the movie went on there was palpable excitement, because it was to be *The French Connection,* and we unhappy few hadn't seen it" (*H,* 172). As fate would have it, the projector broke down, leaving the passengers keenly disappointed. Eager to help, Buckley asked for a screwdriver, notwithstanding the fact that a screwdriver in his hand "is less useful than a computer in the hands of an aborigine" (*H,* 173). After he unscrewed the underside panel and scrutinized the intricate workings of the machine, his "heart sank." It was then that a familiar voice spoke up: "Come on, Bill. Get out of the way. You reactionaries wouldn't know how to fix a broken wheel" (*H,* 173).

Despite their best efforts, neither man was able to fix the projector. Buckley finally gave up when dinner was served, but Humphrey labored on for two more hours, until "he climbed wearily down, and exuberantly attacked his cold dinner" (*H,* 174). Moments later, the plane landed. Remembering that event, Buckley writes: "My companion, they say, is headed for another touchdown, under the guidance of other hands, but they will look after him, I feel certain, and smile at his inability to fix the machine on the 747, merely one more in a long series of terrestrial failures, but God knows he tried." (*H,* 174).

Chapter Eleven
The Polemicist at Play

In his 1976 sailing memoir *Airborne: A Sentimental Journey,* William Buckley tells us that in 1965 he "disappeared surreptitiously from the race for Mayor of New York in order to participate in the [sea] race from Marblehead, Massachusetts, to Halifax, Nova Scotia."[1] That offhand disclosure reveals much about Buckley in particular and, I suspect, about conservatism in general. Whereas the hard left tends to see politics as the most important—if not the only—human activity, conservatives are likely to regard it as a distraction from more sublime endeavors. Indeed, even before Buckley's truancy from the New York mayoral election, Russell Kirk inferred that his friend "would prefer yachting to polemicizing" (*R,* 12).

Implicit here is the libertarian notion that, if only government would get out of the way, men would be free to enjoy life. For the conservative, as for the Marxist, the ideal society is one in which the state has withered away upon the cessation of class warfare. Conservatives, however, do not believe that that blessed event will come about through the dictatorship of the proletariat, but through the proles' learning to accept their station in life (or at least through their forsaking *political* means for elevating themselves from that station). In the meantime, those who seek to preserve a higher dream must occasionally descend into the political arena, if only to hasten the arrival of that happy day when men will race not for office but for port.

The Tree of the Poet

Frequently libertarian and traditionalist conservatives find themselves at odds over the social responsibilities of corporate capitalism. Extreme advocates of laissez-faire seem to think that business makes a sufficient contribution to the public good simply by earning a profit, while those who pay greater homage to Edmund Burke than to Adam Smith bemoan the carnage suffered by communities which have been touched by the invisible hand of commerce. For this reason, some of the most strident critiques of the technocratic ethos have come from the right rather than from the left. (The Agrarian manifesto *I'll Take My Stand* is an obvious, though hardly unique, case in point.) As a country squire who is also an enthusiast for the free market, Bill Buckley is in the precarious position of revering the natural beauty which unfettered capitalism frequently threatens to destroy. In his July 1966 essay "The Politics of Beauty" (*J*, 231–46), Buckley attempts to find a philosophical rationale by which to adjudicate the conflict between those who wish to enjoy God's handiwork and those who wish to make a buck.

Although this conflict has received much greater publicity since the advent of the ecology movement, it was a topic of discussion in the Sharon, Connecticut household of William F. Buckley, Sr. as far back as the late 1930s. Buckley, Jr. remembers his father's consternation when a large billboard appeared on a previously unviolated stretch of New England landscape. Wishing to please their father, the Buckley offspring volunteered to rise *en masse* and burn the sign down. "My father's allegiances were in conflict," Bill Buckley writes. "On the one hand, he himself had once been a revolutionary, or rather counter-revolutionary, who, as a young man, undertook nothing less than the replacement of the order of things in all Mexico. On the other hand, he was the conservative who believed in law and order. The dialectic did not yield altogether convincing results" (*JE*, 233–34).

Foiled by their father's prohibition of this specific act of civil disobedience, William, Jr. and his siblings simply waited until another offender reared his ugly head. In this case, it was the town grouch, who erected a gaudy Coca-Cola sign over his combination cigar store and soda fountain. Under cover of night, the marauding Buckleys streaked the sign beyond recognition with a bucket of white paint, only to see their foe hoist a new sign in a couple of days. "So he won," Buckley concludes; "but a demonstration of sorts had been made, and now I no longer feel I can theoretically defend what I had a hand in doing at age thirteen; but, come to think of it, the sign is no longer there" (*JE*, 234).

Beginning with the proposition that for many people, himself included, "external harmony is necessary for the repose of the soul" (*JE*, 231), Buckley devotes much of his essay to exploring the difficulties of incorporating that imperative into the political order. Particularly when dealing with the urban landscape, there is the problem of differing aesthetic tastes. If we cannot solve social problems simply by throwing money and caseworkers at them, we certainly cannot eliminate urban blight by throwing money and architects at it. As Buckley points out: "The most galvinizing words recently uttered on the matter of saving America the Beautiful came from the President of the United States [Lyndon Johnson], whose superb French cook, inherited from JFK, recently resigned in despair after the superordination of a dietician from Austin, Texas, who ordered him to serve beets with cream on them at affairs of state. Can a man who thus misorders his own kitchen be trusted to design the Acropolis?" (*JE*, 236).

One also senses Buckley's reluctance to make common cause with those whose concern for environmental harmony is either fetishistic or part of some larger ideological agenda. Although he praises Interior Secretary Stewart Udall's efforts to "maintain oases of natural beauty," he goes on to say that Udall sometimes leaves "the impression that he resents any private dwelling at all, on the ground that it is liable to get in the way of a meandering buffalo" (*JE*, 241). Buckley also chastises the ecological alarmists who seem to get a perverse delight out of predicting imminent apocalypse. "[T]heir gloom is so total," he contends, "as to invoke not the impulse to reform, but the impulse to despair" (*JE*, 243).

Still, Buckley is willing to tolerate a certain amount of environmental zealotry "in an age that very much needs to be reminded of the factor of beauty, natural and man-made" (*JE*, 241). For his own part, he can see ample *conservative* grounds for public action against aesthetic nuisances. Indeed:

The display of hortatory commercial slogans is not covered by the same set of arguments used by the anarchical housebuilder—because the billboards are manifestly not directed at himself, but rather at others who pass by. As such the billboards are acts of aggression—like skywriting—against which the public is entitled, as a matter of privacy, to be protected. If a homeowner desires to construct a huge Coca-Cola sign facing his own homestead rather than the public highway, in order to remind him, every time he looks out his window, that the time has come to pause and be refreshed, he certainly should be left free to do so. But if he wants to face the sign towards us, that is something else, and the big name libertarian theorists should go to work demolishing the billboarders' abuse of the argument of private property (*JE*, 240–41).

A practical means of implementing this theoretical insight would be to use zoning laws, the justification for which is already widely conceded, to restrict particularly egregious assaults upon the aesthetic sensibilities of innocent bystanders. Even here, though, one is dependent on the wisdom and decorum of those with decision-making power. The ultimate solution, of course, would be to inculcate a greater appreciation of beauty into the populace at large. Buckley cites as a paradigm a gentleman refugee from Russia, married to Tolstoi's niece, who, "finding himself impoverished in Paris between the wars, took a job as a bus driver on the condition that he be assigned the route to Chartres, so that he might adore it every day" (*JE,* 245).

Although it is difficult to imagine Bill Buckley as a bus driver, even on the route to Chartres, he is right to suggest that the physical surroundings in which one chooses to live say a good deal about one's temporal spirit (the immortal soul being another matter entirely). To say that beauty does indeed lie in the eye of the beholder is not necessarily to argue for aesthetic relativism. Rather, it is to say that, if no one recognized or cherished beauty, it would have no more impact on human life than the proverbial tree which falls in the middle of the forest. "[T]he integrity of impression made by manifold natural objects," Emerson wrote in *Nature,* "distinguishes the stick of timber of the woodcutter from the tree of the poet."

Sportpolitik

The day has long since passed when sports writing could be confined to sports writers. Even if Michelob's vision of a seven-day weekend has yet to be realized, leisure time in America has expanded to the point where leisure-time activities assume an unprecedented importance. As a result, persons with only a marginal interest in big-time athletics frequently find themselves swept into the periphery of controversies which ensue from the impact of sports upon culture. By the late sixties, not even the aristocratic William Buckley could ignore the nation's obsession with grown men playing little boys' games.

In January 1969, Joe Namath led the New York Jets to an historic upset over the Baltimore Colts in Super Bowl III. Then, in June of that year, he announced that he would retire from professional football rather than comply with Commissioner Pete Rozelle's order to sever his connection with a restaurant which gamblers were known to frequent. Although Namath later capitulated and the incident itself has faded from the memory of all but the hardened trivia buff, Buckley's essay "On Understanding the Difficulties of Joe Namath" (*GL,* 430–39) remains an insightful discussion of the political and ethical dynamics of professional sports. What one remembers about this discussion, however, is not its closely reasoned defense of Rozelle's concern for keeping pro football as circumspect as Caesar's wife; but rather, the deft way in which its author manages to engage his reader and himself with a topic about which he knows and cares very little.[2]

Although the American sports scene has always had its share of eccentrics and playboys, Namath and Muhammad Ali—two quintessential figures of the sixties—seemed to represent a new breed of hero, one who was loved—at least in part—for flaunting his iconoclasm. In this regard, Buckley recalls a temperamental bullfighter who was jeered and booed by his audience one afternoon because of his uncharacteristic clumsiness in handling a bull. When the time came to pay ritual obeisance to the crowd by holding his *capa* aloft, this matador "took off his *capa,* dropped it to the ground, lifted his hand with only the middle finger thrust skyward, and slowly and reverentially turned the ceremonial circle" (*GL,* 439). This gesture won the crowd over even as the police rushed into the arena to drag the offender off to jail. And "all night long, the fans serenaded him outside the jailhouse and passed him up myrrh and honey" (*GL,* 439).

In September 1972, Buckley's attention was once again directed to sports; this time not to a single flamboyant personality like Broadway Joe, but to three incongruous events which transpired in the course of a fortnight: the Olympic victory of Russia over the United States in basketball; the triumph of amateur Russian hockey players over Canadian professionals; and the defeat of Russian chess master Boris Spassky by American Bobby Fischer.[3] Given the inevitable politicizing of international sports, each of these anomalies seems fraught with significance.

The two stunning Soviet upsets, Buckley contends, are evidence of certain advantages which a closed and fraudulent society enjoys over open and honest ones. Not only did Eastern-bloc officials rob the United States basketball team of victory, but any contest with Russian amateurs is inherently unfair because of the *de facto* professional status of those "amateurs." That such a point has been made so often as to become tiresome is itself noteworthy: "Not only is it generally true that Communists do *not* tire of being the butt of criticism, it is also true that Westerners *do* tire of offering criticism. Thus you will not only not wear down the Soviet representatives of the Olympic committee by documenting the professional care and feeding of their competitors; you will simultaneously wear down the Americans who level the charges" (*EE,* 240).

If basketball is endemic to the United States and hockey to Canada, chess must be regarded as the national game of Russia. It is, therefore, only poetic justice that, at the same time the Russians were experiencing unprecedented success in Western sports, their own hegemony in chess be shattered by a brash young American. According to Buckley, Bobby Fischer treated "Borississimo Spassky the way old Iron Butt Molotov treated the Western powers over nearly a generation. No. No. No. No. No! The square was too square, the circle too round, the line too straight. . . . [H]e made his demands and discovered (what others have less conspicuously discovered) that when one wishes to prevail against the Soviet Union, the best way to do it is to assert oneself" (*EE,* 244). That this lesson was never transferred from chess to diplomacy is something for which the Soviets can be thankful. Had Bobby Fischer been our chief SALT negotiator, such phrases as "window of vulnerability" might never have been coined.

For reasons that sociologists will be debating for years to come, the 1970s proved to be boom years in American sports. (Among other things free agentry in professional athletics made even overrated mediocrities like Reggie Jackson into wealthy media personalities, while a wave of cultural nostalgia transformed heroes of yesterday into elegiac cult figures.) Never one to miss a social trend, *Esquire* published a special "Super Sports Issue" in October 1974. Although most of the contributors were men learned in sports lore, the introductory essay was written by William Buckley—a commentator whose childhood idol was not Joltin' Joe or the Brown Bomber or even Frank Merriwell, but a wicked baton twirler named Arturo Toscanini.

Calling his essay "Reflections on the Phenomenon" (*EE,* 217–27), Buckley ponders the atavistic enthusiasm which sports can generate in otherwise sane and sober persons. He suspects, for example, that the very concreteness of athletic achievement may have something to do with the esteem in which it is held: "Joe DiMaggio is up at bat not necessarily more often than Toscanini, but the results are easier to chart, and they appear in the next morning's newspapers and the next year's almanacs. DiMaggio's home runs were discretely recorded; Toscanini's merely accumulated a little more density in the aurora borealis that hovered over his name" (*EE,* 218–19). Also, there is the element of vicarious identification. People tend to feel that "DiMaggio was just that little critical step better than Johnny, who concededly is not a member of the same human family that produced Einstein or Freud" (*EE,* 219).

Not quite satisfied with these explanations, Buckley explores the connection between sports mania and tribal loyalties. In our increasingly deracinated age, sports heroes become symbolic warriors who remind us of our social identity. Not only do local residents cheer on the hometown team, but Catholics root for Notre Dame. At crucial points in their struggle for social equality, blacks identified themselves with Joe Louis over Max Schmeling and women with Billie Jean King over Bobby Riggs. Even the Red Chinese love their ping pong players and greet them more warmly than they do the likes of Chou En-Lai.

Finally, it may be that athletic competition is the one area of modern life where people still uniformly revere excellence. When college football coaches are paid two to three times as much as a school's most distinguished professor, there can hardly be any doubt about what is the most important activity on campus. And Babe Ruth's legendary remark that he made more money than the President of the United States because he had had a better year than the President ceases to amuse only because it is now commonplace for sports stars to outearn and outperform presidents. But even if society should one day cease to reward athletic achievement, perhaps a self-sustaining spark still will animate sportsmen to attain their personal best, just as the spark of art and intellect animated another kind of achievement during the Dark Ages. Indeed, should this be the case, "we will know that though the pulse is very low, it continues to beat, and to tap out a stimulus that is ultimately more exciting than the second hand of a stopwatch or a locomotive cheer on the crowded sidelines" (*EE*, 227).

O Captain, My Captain

If Buckley's credentials for pontificating on the traumas of Joe Namath, the politics of international sports, and the sociology of athletic competition are vaguely suspect, he is in more familiar waters when extolling the joys and challenges of sailing. Although his essays on the subject go back as far as *Rumbles Left and Right* (1964), he seems to have made a more or less definitive statement in *Airborne: A Sentimental Journey* (1976). An account of his voyage from Miami, Florida, to Marbella, Spain, aboard the schooner Cyrano, this reminiscence is—according to Buckley—"the only thing I have ever written that everyone liked"(*H,* 18).[4]

Because of the enthusiastic response which it evoked, we might do well to inquire into the appeal of this sailing memoir. (Indeed, since many of the people who liked the book had never been on a sailboat, Buckley is himself perplexed by *Airborne*'s popularity.) I suspect that what we have here is an instance of America's obsession with the private lives of public men. Particularly since the advent of television, we have come to regard national celebrities as familiar presences.[5] For this reason, our natural curiosity about them is no longer restrained by the reticence which we would feel in the presence of kings or popes. If Bill Buckley can come to our breakfast tables three times a week in his newspaper column and to our living rooms once a week in his television show, then—by God—we ought to be allowed on his yacht. And in *Airborne* he welcomes us aboard.

Those who come to this book expecting to find a lyrical meditation on man in nature are likely to be disappointed.[6] (Buckley is no Izaak Walton or Peter Matthiessen, and he is certainly no Herman Melville.) What we get instead is an aquatic comedy of manners—a sort of saltwater sitcom. The principals are Buckley himself, good buddy Evan Galbraith, sister-in-law Kathleen ("Bill") Finucane, son Christopher, and son Christopher's friend Danny Merritt. These five and a few crew members set out to cross the Atlantic—no doubt because it is there.

In order to provide background for this voyage, Buckley tells us of his many adventures and misadventures away from land. If he does not exactly come across as a klutz, he is—at the very least—victimized by the caprice of nature and the enigma of technology. While sailing with young Bill on separate occasions during his adolescence, a classmate and a sister almost drowned. Later on, one of his yachts sank while sitting in the Stamford, Connecticut boatyard. Then, there is the time that he miscalculated the tides on St. John's River in New Brunswick and nearly landed in the middle of an Esso station.

Probably the most heartrending story in this litany, however, occurs during the annual Martha's Vineyard Race. As he is taking his watch in the middle of a foggy night, Buckley is able to discern "a few lights . . . , a stern light, and masthead light, and perhaps a flash-light" (*A,* 65). "We're overhauling that poor bastard!" his friend Mike Mitchell exults as both men feel "the special pleasure of sliding by a competitor." "Mike was right," Buckley recalls. "We were getting closer and closer. I checked the compass—dead on the course I had stipulated. I eased the bow the slightest bit up to make certain we would be comfortably to windward of the boat. Then came the screech, the ricocheting crunch of steel bouncing over rocks and, in a moment, motionlessness. . . . A hundred yards away was the boat we were pursuing, now plainly visible. Two forlorn street lights, one mile north of Port Judith. We were two miles off course" (*A,* 65).

Given Buckley's mishaps at sea, it is little wonder that his long-suffering wife Pat prefers to stay on land. Playing Blondie to Bill's Dagwood, Pat Buckley serves as a standard of normalcy and intuitive common sense against which to measure her husband's wanderlust. Early in their cruising career (Mrs. Buckley refuses to race), the polemicist convinced his wife that a sailboat will almost always right itself. Nevertheless, he tells us, the second day out on Cyrano's predecesor *The Panic*: "I noticed a two-inch section of that omnipresent plastic tape on which you punch out labels and the like. It was pegged on the circumference of the boat's inclinometer, a two-dollar piece of hardware you tack on the cockpit bulkhead. Its loose-floated pendulum indicates on an arc the angle of the boat's heel at any given moment. It read, opposite the 25° point on the scale: 'PATSY GETS OFF'" (*A*, 56).

Early in *Airborne*, its author recalls an experience from years past which involved himself, his wife, and their six-year-old son. In an effort to entertain young Chrisopher, his parents buried ten-dollars worth of costume jewelry on an island near their home. With the aid of an authentic-looking pirate map, the lad located this booty, which he lovingly turned over to his mother. This required her—whenever her son was around—to wear a full suit of Woolworth jewelry. However, there were also occasions when people other than her son were around. These people "clearly wondered what on earth had happened to the taste in jewelry of the chic and stunning Mrs. Buckley" (*A*, 6).

When Christopher decided to return to the island later that summer to search for further treasure, Buckley concluded that the ideal expedient would be to bury four or five of Pat's Georgian silver pieces. (These she could exhibit in company without embarrassment.) So, armed with an elaborate new map, Christopher and his friend Danny proceeded to the enchanted island. Unfortunately, three days and Hurricane Hilda intervened between the burying of the treasure and the boys' attempt to locate it. After two hours and six excavations, that attempt was abandoned as futile. Just as futile were Buckley's efforts to placate his understandably irate wife. "We tried a half dozen times over the next months to find the buried casket," he writes. "It is still there, somewhere" (*A*, 6).

Aboard Cyrano in the mid-Atlantic with a crew of hardy men and a sister-in-law named Bill, Buckley is temporarily freed from what Washington Irving called "petticoat government." The focus of domestic interest thus shifts from the relationship of husband and wife to that of father and son. Assuming the role of adoring but exasperated parent, Buckley comments on everything from Christopher's beard ("he began the trip looking like Peter Pan and ended by looking like Charles Manson" [*A,* 141]) to his behavior on shore ("I have wondered whether it is tradition or biological compulsion that requires sailors, on reaching shore, to go berserk. Whatever the answer, Danny and Christopher . . . did not let down the tradition. They seemed to concert perfectly to enact a scene from Henry Miller . . ." [*A,* 217]).

Perhaps an incident which Buckley recounts in the prologue to *Airborne* best exemplifies the abrasive affection which binds the generations. After speaking sharply to Christopher and Danny when the two appeared on board one night without lifebelts, Buckley is filled with remorse. Had he scarred his son emotionally by humiliating him in front of his friend? Hours later, the contrite father decides to go aloft and make peace with the boys before they leave their watch. Prior to doing so, however, he checks the log book. At the end of his last entry, he had written: "Relieved by Capt. Merritt and Lt. Buckley, whose lifebelts were, in due course, located" (*A,* xvii). Reading on to the next line, he is elated. "Everything was all right. The boys had evidently seen my entry. Their indignation was furious, but not internalized. They had made their own entry, using my pen for the purpose:

"'*My ass, Buckley*—DTM.' And from my son, '*Screw you*—CTB.' Nowhere in the vast Atlantic that night was any skipper better pleased with the junior members of his crew, and just think of it, one of them my own flesh and blood" (*A,* xviii). Of such is the Kingdom of Heaven.

Chapter Twelve
The Artist as Critic

Bill Buckley is such a familiar presence on the political landscape that it is necessary to pause and remind ourselves that the man is not a politician. Although he ran for Mayor of New York and served in two appointive positions in the Nixon administration, those activities were mere diversions from his primary vocation. His reputation as an important figure in contemporary American culture must finally rest on his ability to manipulate the English language. Those studying earlier periods of British and American literature are keenly aware that the essayist, just as surely as the novelist and the poet, is a literary artist in his own right. This is no less true in our present age.

Only time will tell whether James Jackson Kilpatrick is correct in arguing that the current generation of syndicated columnists is the equal of Addison and Steele;[1] however, there can be little doubt that Buckley has done much to enhance the literary quality of contemporary journalism. No mere politician could accomplish this feat. What was needed was a commentator whose interests extended over the broad range of humane letters. Buckley filled this role because, as Mitchell S. Ross points out, he is essentially a moralist, "a Catholic romantic, waging a campaign for an aesthetic standard of life."[2]

Superior Craftsmen

Like other artists, and most showmen and athletes, writers are individual practitioners who work within a tradition. Even discounting the question of literary influence, about which Harold Bloom would appear to have had the final word, it should come as no surprise that writers are fans of other writers. When T. S. Eliot dedicated *The Waste Land* to Ezra Pound *il miglior fabbro,* he meant to demonstrate critical judgment rather than personal modesty. Similarly, Buckley's praise of other word merchants tells us much about the qualities of style which he admires. And as former *NR* staffer Joan Didion has observed: "Style is character."[3]

In an age of scientific future shock, one of our few remaining links with the past is the English language itself. Hence, those who attempt to preserve the language are nothing less than cultural heroes. In his December 1971 review of *The Compact Edition of the Oxford English Dictionary,* Buckley salutes an act of group heroism. "[T]o use the words of its publishers in connection with the new edition," he writes, the *O.E.D.* is "'the most prestigious book ever published,' even as the moon-landing is almost indisputably the most prestigious scientific enterprise ever consummated" (*I,* 389). Unlike scientific enterprises, however, a cultural achievement like the *O.E.D.* is not rendered obsolescent by the next rocket launch.

Buckley gives us something of the history of this project and then takes out his magnifying glass to peer at the microprint and quote a 400-word explanation of the proper use of the hyphen. With an almost sexual ardor that most of the rest of us reserve for such things as the unsplit infinitive and the serial comma, he exults: "Is that not beautiful? One can read it again and again, once for the analysis, again as philosophy, twice more for the music; and there isn't an entry in the dictionary that does not present itself as manifestly the object of the lovingcare (note, no hyphen) these grave, and lively, and penetrating craftsmen gave us" (*I,* 392).

Leading the list of Buckley's favorite individual writers is fellow Catholic Tory Evelyn Waugh. Using Holden Caulfield's standard of literary affectiveness, Waugh is the sort of writer whom readers would like to phone up. However, if they did so, the receiver probably would be slammed down at the other end of the line. Although Waugh corresponded with Buckley and even contributed to *National Review,* the two men never met.

As one might expect, Buckley's obituary essay on Waugh is a worshipful appreciation of man and artist. (*JE,* 302–4). Its opening, however, reveals at least as much about Buckley as it does about Waugh. Here, the eulogist remembers encountering an angry lady in Dallas, Texas, whose mission in life was to keep dirty books off the shelves of the local library. In the course of their conversation, the future author of *Saving the Queen* observed that to remove all salacious passages from modern literature would require that each of us have private readers much like an old eccentric in one of Waugh's novels. "Who, asked the lady book critic, is Evelyn Waugh? The greatest English novelist of this century, I ventured;

but, on ascertaining that he was not a dirty writer, she lost all interest and went off to look for more dirty books to rail against" (*JE,* 303). One wonders what this lady might have thought of the highly suggestive PBS production of Waugh's *Brideshead Revisited,* a series whose host was William F. Buckley, Jr.

Although it might seem a light-year's journey from the world of Evelyn Waugh to that of Tom Wolfe, both men can be regarded as consummately deft conservative satirists. (Indeed, Wolfe's *Radical Chic* is arguably a Manhattan version of Waugh's *Black Mischief.*) One other thing which these two writers have in common is the admiration of Bill Buckley. In December 1970, Buckley declared Wolfe to be "probably the most skillful writer in America" (*I,* 349) and then went on to give a marvellously apt description of his subject's style: "He is like the pianist Henry Scott, who can play 'Flight of the Bumblebee' while wearing mittens" (*I,* 349).

Understandably, Buckley takes particular pleasure in Wolfe's pyrotechnics when they are used to expose liberal fatuity. What is becoming increasingly apparent as the years go by, however, is that Wolfe's narrative aesthetic is even more traditional than his social vision. Underneath all the glitter, Wolfe is essentially a Victorian novelist who disdains the postrealist innovations of modernism. As such, he is to the literary right of such *NR* contributors as Guy Davenport, Hugh Kenner, Jeffrey Hart, and D. Keith Mano.

If Buckley's affinity for Waugh and Wolfe makes obvious sense, his affection for Norman Mailer may strike some as aberrant. Indeed, anyone who has heard Buckley and Mailer go after each other in public debate might naively conclude that the two men were bitter enemies. And yet, Mailer explains: "Buckley and I are like wrestlers. . . . One night we wrestle in Atlantic City, then we go out for a beer together, and the next night we're at it again in Pittsburgh."[4] Despite declaring Mailer "in every categorical sense . . . an utter and hopeless mess" (*JE,* 224), Buckley "love[s] him as an artist . . . [because] he makes the most beautiful metaphors in the business, as many as a dozen of them on a single page worth anthologizing" (*JE,* 223).

In addition to his ability to make metaphors, what fascinates Buckley about Mailer is the suspicion that "as a philosopher, . . . [he] is—dare I say it?—in his own fashion, a conservative." "Wrestling in the twentieth century with the hegemonies of government and ideology," Buckley continues, "the conservative tends to side with the individualist" (*JE,* 224). That Mailer is an individualist can hardly be denied. He may even refer to himself as a left-conservative. However, what this amounts to is less traditional conservatism than antiliberal, antirationalist romanticism. Although such a stance is not without its appeal for Buckley, he and Mailer are still philosophically poles apart. At his most avant-garde Buckley is a Bohemian Tory; at his most staid Mailer is a Tory Bohemian.

Mailer is not the only literary man of the left whom Buckley reveres. Throughout most of his tenure in public life, he and columnist Murray Kempton have carried on a good-natured rivalry. Indeed, surveying the candidates for Mayor of New York in 1965 (a year in which he supported John Lindsay), Kempton remarked: "The only one in the group I would dare call collect long distance for a loan is William F. Buckley, Jr." (*U*, 366). Whether or not he would accept charges, Buckley pays Kempton a number of professional compliments in "A Fortnight with Murray Kempton" (*R*, 132–43).

This essay is basically a selection of two weeks' worth of Kempton's commentary (rendered in italics), complete with observations and digressions by Buckley. Despite their ideological differences, Buckley and Kempton both have the facility to make transient controversies memorable by virtue of the wit and grace with which they write about them. Who, today, cares about the fact that New York Mayor Robert Wagner once hired a $40,000-a-year public relations team? But who can fail to be impressed by Kempton's reaction to this move: "[Wagner] *is the full flower of Mencken's law that no man ever went broke underestimating the intelligence of the American voter. I resent having to pay taxes for press agents to protect a man whose magnificent effrontery already makes him invulnerable.*" As Buckley observes: "There aren't six men in the country who could have composed that last sentence" (*R*, 135).

Kempton is able to get away with as much as he does because he is personally well liked. According to Buckley: "He has no trouble at all mixing easily with those whom the next morning he will berate with a passionate wit. As a matter of fact, K has no enemies, and that is an unusual estate for a man with so forked and active a tongue" (*R*, 140). Indeed, he is probably the only writer to contribute concurrently to *National Review* and the *New York Review of Books*. Kempton has said of his friend that at times "Buckley tempts you to remember Macauley's grudging compliment to Burke, which was that he generally chose his side like a fanatic and defended it like a philosopher" (*U*, 366). Buckley might well return the compliment. Although he may disagree with what Kempton says, he will applaud to the death the way in which Kempton says it.

Arts and Manners

It hardly seems to follow as a matter of logical necessity that cultural conservatism should have political overtones. And yet, in the 1960s, a significant percentage of the nation's self-important youth saw itself as a distinct counterculture, in rebellion against adult mores in dress, grooming, music, and politics. Because of the postwar baby boom, the adolescent population of the sixties was disproportionately large. At the same time, national prosperity gave youth the leisure to question the values of their parents. As a result, long hair, rock music, drugs, and opposition to the Vietnam War became identified in the public mind as part of the same syndrome. In 1968, this new barbarism was celebrated in a rock musical called *Hair.*

Bill Buckley's response to *Hair* was to praise it guardedly on artistic grounds—"The music and action are engagingly energetic" (*GL,* 403)—while deploring it philosophically. Ultimately, however, his reaction is less one of outrage than of weary condescension: "The obscenities fail somehow to shock. The nudity is less remarkable by far than the posturings at the stripper joint" (*GL,* 403). *Hair* succeeded only in dramatizing what most people already knew—that "youth is very mixed up." Despite, or perhaps because, of this fact, it is "the responsibility of the adult world . . . to hang on to one's sanity." Buckley concludes that "seeing *Hair* makes one a little prouder of middle-class establishmentarian standards" (*GL,* 404).

Another theatrical production which helped confirm Buckley's belief in the virtue of stodginess was the 1974 film *Lenny.* A disingenuously laudatory treatment of the life of comedian Lenny Bruce, this picture pandered to the notion that Bruce was a martyr and prophet. However, the self-inflicted suffering of drug addiction does not constitute martyrdom, nor does the exploitation of dirty words constitute prophecy. In an apt comparison, Buckley notes that "reading De Sade now is like reading pathology, and listening to Lenny Bruce is like a visit to one of those clinics where they keep two-headed children until, mercifully, they die off" (*EE,* 403).

Buckley is not arguing for censorship, but neither does he buy the notion that a belief in free speech requires us to suspend our critical sensibilities. When Bruce is being self-indulgent, gratuitously cruel, or just plain unfunny, one should not refrain from saying so for fear of being classed with the book-burners and the know-nothings. Buckley is willing to feel sorry, though not too sorry, for Lenny Bruce. What he is unwilling to do is to join the hagiographers who regard this foul-mouthed junkie as a social satirist in the tradition of Swift and Twain.

Of course, social iconoclasm is not confined to such obvious bohemian types as the flower children of *Hair* and Lenny Bruce. In recent years, a more genteel dissent from traditional middle-class values has become so fashionable as to be the new norm. In the vanguard of this social transformation is Helen Gurley Brown and her magazine *Cosmopolitan*. A conservative by philosophy and a gadfly by temperament, Bill Buckley can hardly be expected to resist so tempting a target.

Just as he praises Murray Kempton through selective quotation, Buckley uses this same technique to expose the essential shallowness and absurdity of Mrs. Brown's pseudochic posturings. Consider, for example, the following revelation: "Are you, sir, a breast fetishist? I mean, *madam*, is your *lover* a breast fetishist? Don't despair. Don't go away. Hear what *Jill* did. *Cosmo* reveals that on her wedding night she *'came to bed with a big dollop of Hershey's milk-chocolate syrup tipping each breast. Honest! Stan is still a fetishist. But his fetish is his wife. And they keep a can of Hershey's by the bed. Does that hurt anyone?'"* (*I*, 373–74).

If *Cosmopolitan* preaches the gospel of sexual liberation, it stops short of the ideal of women's liberation. The *Cosmopolitan* girl is not less interested in getting a man than is the heroine of a Jane Austen novel; she just goes about it more crudely. "As HGB puts it, *'You've got to make yourself more cupcakeable all the time so that you're a better cupcake to be gobbled up'"* (*I*, 374). The doctrine of Helen Gurley Brown is less remarkable than the seriousness and the intensity with which it is proclaimed. Upon learning that a *Cosmopolitan* staff member and her husband live in a renovated church, Buckley remarks: "But of course! The whole of *Cosmopolitan* has become a renovated church" (*I*, 373).

"What do Mary McCarthy, Joyce Carol Oates, Muriel Spark, and Joan Didion have in common?" Buckley asks at the beginning of another column (*H*, 293). The answer is that they are all first-class writers who happen to be women (as opposed to the patronizing "first-class women writers"). Moreover, precisely because these women are such fine prose stylists, they "would shun like the plague such exhortations as are being urged on all writers by the National Council of Teachers of English (NCTE), in the name of eliminating sexism" (*H*, 293).

Although the criticism which Buckley levels at the NCTE may seem mild when compared to the invective of John Simon, there is no question that he holds this organization in the contempt which it so richly merits. Not only would the neuterization of the language desecrate our literary heritage, he argues, but it would also promote syntactical awkwardness and imprecision and, in some cases, even faulty pronoun agreement. It is perhaps to be expected that such Orwellian bowdlerization would be urged by dogmatic feminists. What is inexcusable is that those who should be guarding the language have gone over to the enemy. This is one issue on which Buckley is unquestionably on the side of civilization.

Traditional grammar is not the only social convention which has come under attack from militant egalitarians. Another casualty of the leveling process is the custom of addressing all but one's most intimate friends in formal terms. This dying amenity is one which the courtly Mr. Buckley is eager to preserve. On *Firing Line,* for example, he continues to refer even to long-time acquaintances as "Mr. Burnham," or "Senator Goldwater," or (prior to his more recent elevation) "Governor Reagan." "The effort, I thought, was worthwhile," he writes, "—a small gesture against the convention that requires you to refer to Professor Mortimer Applegate as 'Mort' five minutes after you have met. Jack Paar would have called Socrates 'Soc'" (*H,* 308).

And yet, in resisting the first-name trend, one runs the risk of appearing insufferably stuffy. (For this reason, Buckley finally stopped referring to the host of the *Tonight Show* as "Mr. Carson." As he discovered: "Mr. Carson does not exist in America. Only Johnny does" [*H,* 308].) A corollary of this problem is the social pressure to be "One of the Boys." Fearing this "more than anything except rattlesnakes and détente," Buckley observes: "'Just call me Bill' to the roommate of your son at college, is in my judgment an odious effort to efface a chronological interval as palpable as the wrinkles on my face, and the maturity of my judgments" (*H,* 308–9). A solution which Dick Cavett proposed to Buckley was to adopt the Southern habit of prefacing first names with "Mister." This expedient, however, might result in "Mr. Bill" and "Mr. Dick" being mistaken, respectively, for William Faulkner and a character out of Dickens.[5]

Surely the most memorable scene in Paddy Chayevsky's *Network* is the one in which Peter Finch, in the role of an enraged anchorman, exhorts his listeners to open their windows and scream: "I'm mad as hell and I'm not going to take it anymore." William Buckley touches on much the same nerve in the final entry of *Rumbles Left and Right,* an essay entitled "Why Don't We Complain."

"[W]e are all increasingly anxious in America to be unobtrusive," Buckley writes, "we are reluctant to make our voices heard, hesitant about claiming our rights" (*R,* 188). These words are directed to the average reader in reference to the average daily annoyances. The personal experiences which Buckley cites include being forced to sit in a railway car heated to 85 degrees when the temperature outdoors was below freezing; being subjected to a two-hour motion picture which was slightly out of focus; and being poorly served by incompetent waitresses and airline stewardesses. What irks Buckley is not so much that our lives are made more exasperating by the behavior of knaves and fools as that we are meek enough to take it. (Viewing the film *Five Easy Pieces,* the audience invariably applauds when Jack Nicholson flies into a rage at a waitress who will not serve him a sandwich which can be easily fixed but which is not on the menu. As he sends plates and silverware crashing to the floor, the Walter Mitty in all of us stands a little taller.)

The ability to put up with vexations which cannot be corrected is a sign of maturity; however, the willingness to endure those which can be corrected is a sign of decadence. And the long-range consequences of such decadence can be profound. "When our voices are finally mute, when we have finally suppressed the natural instinct to complain, whether the vexation is trivial or grave, we shall have become automatons, incapable of feeling" (*R,* 191). As Pogo so sagely observed: "We have met the enemy and he is us."

The Odd Couple

Appearing on the *Merv Griffin Show* sometime in the early seventies (I neglected to note the date), Gore Vidal was asked why his engagement to Joanne Woodward never resulted in marriage. "She met Paul Newman," Vidal replied, "and I met William Buckley." Although the relationship of Vidal and Buckley has been considerably less amorous, though arguably no less passionate, than that of Newman and Woodward, the former "couple" is at least as indissolubly linked in the public mind as is the latter. It is a noteworthy irony that two such bitter opponents as Vidal and Buckley should have done so much to publicize each other.

The bad blood between the two polemicists goes back to 1962, when Vidal, appearing on the *Jack Paar Show,* mentioned Buckley's name as part of a little homily he was delivering about the danger on the right. The following evening Buckley was afforded equal time to reply. Then, on the third night, Vidal returned to level more charges (several of which were distorted) against both William and the entire Buckley clan. In an effort to defend the honor of his family, Brother Bill came very close to sending the following telegram to Parr: "Please inform Gore Vidal that neither I nor my family is disposed to receive lessons in morality from a pink queer. If he wishes to challenge that designation, inform him that I shall fight by the laws of the Marquis of Queensbury. He will know what I mean." As Charles Lam Markmann notes: this telegram "was at once unpardonable and yet craftsmanlike in the nice aptness of its allusion to a past scandal in the literary world."[6]

Six years later, during one of the most turbulent years in the history of American politics, ABC television decided to spice up its coverage of the 1968 Republican and Democratic conventions by featuring live commentary from Buckley and Vidal. The ensuing rhetorical bloodbath did little to enhance the prestige of either participant and proved a major setback for civilized discourse.

Because he was better prepared for the confrontation and took it more seriously, the liberal spokesman piled up an early lead. Armed with quotations from the major candidates and from Buckley himself, Vidal attempted to smother his opponent with a barrage of facts and accusations. It is a hard strategy to defend against, because, if one seeks to respond at length to any single charge, he gives the impression of simultaneously ducking ten others. Seeing that Vidal had him off-balance, Buckley tried to seize the initiative by making gratuitous references to his foe's recent best-seller *Myra Breckinridge*. As a result, Vidal did better than one might have expected against a more experienced political commentator. The fact that Buckley had broken his shoulder in a boating accident hardly improved his disposition.

As the running cat fight proceeded from the Republican Convention in Miami to the Democratic in Chicago, Buckley regained his poise and managed to needle Vidal on several occasions. One particularly memorable exchange occurred when Buckley produced a letter he had received from the late Robert Kennedy. In part, it read: "I have changed my platform for 1968 from 'Let's give blood to the Vietcong' to 'Let's give Gore Vidal to the Vietcong.'"[7] Indeed, Buckley scored well the couple of times he managed to invoke the name of the recently martyred Bobby in the presence of the anti-Kennedy Vidal. (At the very least, it was a far more effective tactic than were the *ad hominem* attacks on the "author of *Myra Breckinridge*.")

On the night of the celebrated police riot, when demonstrators, newsmen, and innocent bystanders were indiscriminately mugged by Mayor Daley's stormtroopers, the tempers in the television booth were even shorter than usual. The subject of Nazism was interjected into the discussion when moderator Howard K. Smith suggested an analogy between hoisting a Vietcong flag in Chicago and displaying Nazi colors during World War II. Feeling that the police and their defenders had more affinities with the Gestapo than did Abbie Hoffman and company, Vidal sneered at Buckley: *"As far as I am concerned, the only crypto Nazi I can think of is yourself, failing that, I would only say that we can't have. . . ."* At that point, Buckley delivered the substance of the telegram he had failed to send half-a-dozen years earlier: *"Now listen, you queer. Stop calling me a crypto Nazi or I'll sock you in your goddamn face and you'll stay plastered."*[8] "It was a splendid moment," Vidal recalls. "Eyes rolling, mouth twitching, long weak arms waving, [Buckley] skittered from slander to glorious absurdity. 'I was,' he honked, 'in the Infantry in the last war.'"[9]

Rather than quitting while they were just a little bit behind, Buckley and Vidal published lengthy apologias in *Esquire* and then promptly sued each other for libel. Vidal's suit, based on the contention that Buckley had committed slander by calling him a pornographer and a producer of perverted prose, was thrown out on the ground that the comments in question fell within the province of literary criticism. Buckley, however, proved more successful, in that he managed to extract both an apology and reimbursement for $115,000 in legal expenses from *Esquire*. He then folded his hand by dropping his suit against Vidal, leaving the latter with $75,000 in *unreimbursed* legal bills.

The charge that Bill Buckley is a "crypto-Nazi" is neither accurate nor polite; however, it is no more inherently libellous than some of the charges which *National Review* has lodged against well-known men of the left. When Linus Pauling sued *NR* for calling him a fellow traveler (the left-wing equivalent of a "crypto-Nazi"), the court ruled that as a public figure he was fair game for such criticism. However, Vidal was not content simply to make vague slurs about Buckley's political sympathies.

In his *Esquire* article, Vidal sought to document Buckley's "crypto-Nazi" leanings by resurrecting an ancient family scandal. Specifically, Vidal charges that in 1944 a Sharon, Connecticut Episcopal church was vandalized because the real-estate agent who had recently admitted the first Jewish family to the community happened to be the rector's wife. According to Vidal, three Buckley siblings were convicted of this crime. What he fails to point out is that two non-Buckleys were involved—one Protestant and one Jewish—and that the prank arose out of a quarrel with the rector's daughter, not his wife. Moreover, William was not among the group, but at the time was in South Carolina waiting to be drafted into the army to fight *against* Nazism. In any event, to hold one responsible for the behavior of other members of one's family is quite simply slander by association, the sort of thing that liberals were so exercised at Joe McCarthy for practicing. As Vidal no doubt knows, a nephew of Thomas Jefferson's once butchered an uppity slave for breaking one of his mother's prized pitchers. And yet, not even Vidal's Aaron Burr tries to tie this unpleasantness to Jefferson himself.

When he dropped his suit against Vidal, Buckley expressed the hope that the experience would teach his nemesis "to observe the laws of libel." If anything, it may have taught him to circumvent those laws more adroitly. In his 1973 novel *Burr,* Vidal creates a character named William de la Touche Clancey. Clancey is a Tory whose "voice is like that of a furious goose, all honks and hisses." We learn that Clancey "detests our democracy, finds even the Whigs radical, the Adams family vulgar, Daniel Webster a *sans coulotte.* He fills the pages of his magazine *America* with libellous comments on all things American. Despite a rich wife and five children, he is a compulsive sodomite, forever preying on country boys new to the city."[10] In an afterword, Vidal disingenuously notes that "William de la Touche Clancey . . . could, obviously, be based on no one at all."[11]

When Norman Mailer felt himself slandered by Vidal, he took direct measures to settle the account. Walking up to Mr. Myra Breckinridge at a 1977 party, Mailer threw a drink in his face and landed a sucker punch. This display prompted *NR* staffer Joe Sobran to write the following memo to his editor: "Others talk. Mailer acts."[12]

Chapter Thirteen
How the West Was Saved

From timely exposés of existing social ills to utopian projections of what Tennyson called "a newer world," much of American literature has been animated by a desire for social reform. Conversely, reform itself frequently has been furthered, shaped, and even initiated by the exhortations of the printed word. Indeed, the very founding of the American nation consisted not only of a dissolution of political ties with Great Britain, but also—because of "a decent respect for the opinions of mankind"—of an articulation of the reasons for that dissolution. And as America has continued, over the years, to invent and reinvent itself,[1] the literature of social protest has played an integral role in the ongoing process of national self-definition.

It is conceivable that an outsider who knew nothing of this country other than what he read in its protest literature might envision America as a nation perpetually seething with dissent, ready at any moment to erupt into revolutionary conflict. Unfortunately, we do not have a large body of conservative belles lettres with which to counterbalance such a one-sided view of our national life. Although it would be difficult to cite a definitive reason for the relative paucity of right-wing imaginative literature, several plausible explanations suggest themselves.

To begin with, most writers—to the extent that they have identifiable political opinions—tend to be left of center. In a pragmatic, bourgeois, materialistic culture, an artistically serious writer frequently is regarded as, at best, effete and eccentric and, at worst, degenerate and subversive. In turn, that writer himself will often repudiate the culture from which he has been ostracized. As trite as it may seem, the image of the alienated artist is not altogether inaccurate.

Moreover, those writers who are conservative tend not to be right-wing activists, but persons who are deeply skeptical about politics. For that reason, their writing generally focuses on nonpolitical topics. It would be extremely difficult, for example, to discern from their literary efforts that

Wallace Stevens was a Taft Republican or that Jack Kerouac was a *National Review* conservative. Even if one is looking for a critique of left totalitarianism, he would be well advised to ignore the work of conservative writers in favor of the novels of such avowed socialists as George Orwell and Arthur Koestler.

If there is a conservative literary tradition, it is to be found not in imaginative writing but in the prose essay. Some of the most insightful and provocative work in recent literary criticism has been done by conservatives like Hugh Kenner, Guy Davenport, Russell Kirk, Duncan Williams, and various members of the Nashville school of new critics. Furthermore, in the social and cultural journalism of Tom Wolfe, Joan Didion, George F. Will, R. Emmett Tyrrell, and William Buckley himself, one finds highly literate critiques of liberal orthodoxy.

Those who wish to find a body of belle lettres informed by a conservative or right-wing muse must settle in contemporary America for the works of the later Dos Passos and those of Ayn Rand, Allen Drury, and Taylor Caldwell. Although Macell D. Ezell in his book *Unequivocal Americanism*[2] adds a few names to this list (for example, those of Holmes Alexander, Stephen C. Shadegg, D. Keith Mano, and Bill's brother F. Reid Buckley), none of these novelists is likely ever to be as well known or as highly regarded as—say—John Steinbeck or Norman Mailer. It was therefore a significant development when William F. Buckley, probably the most prominent conservative spokesman in America today, announced to the world—as did old Razzia in *Stained Glass*—that in addition to all else, he would "also write novels."

Boffing the Queen

In *Saving the Queen* (1976), *Stained Glass* (1978), *Who's On First* (1980), and *Marco Polo, If You Can* (1982), Buckley takes us back to the Cold War years of the 1950s. We see those times through the eyes of Blackford Oakes, a young Adonis turned CIA agent.[3] Like his creator, Oakes is a veteran of World War II and a graduate of Yale. Indeed, the biographical similarities between author and protagonist are so striking that one is tempted to conclude that Blackford is Buckley's Walter Mitty image of himself.

Like Blackford, Buckley served in the CIA during the early 1950s; however, unlike Oakes, he remained in the agency only seven or eight months and was stationed, not in Europe, but in Mexico. During this time his immediate superior in the spy organization was future Watergate conspirator and fellow novelist E. Howard Hunt. (Hunt, trivia buffs may recall, made such a hit with his first novel *East of Farewell* [1943] that he was awarded a Guggenheim fellowship, beating out—among other applicants—Truman Capote and Gore Vidal.)

We first meet the dashing young Oakes in *Saving the Queen,* where we see him recruited into the CIA and set up as a deep-cover agent in London. His mission is to find out who in the inner circle of the court has been passing H-bomb secrets to the Russians. In the process he penetrates Windsor Castle, the Queen's boudoir, and the royal person of Queen Caroline herself (Elizabeth II and her younger sister perished in a plane crash, thus paving the way for the coronation of Buckley's fictitious queen).

As it turns out, the Soviet spy is the Queen's second cousin and oldest friend Viscount Peregrine Kirk. An ace flier during World War II, Kirk is assigned after the war to a command post in Palestine where he sees terrorism at close range. He eventually returns to England and suffers severe injuries when he falls from his horse while participating in the 1948 Olympics. During his convalescence, he is cared for by a nurse who reads to him from the works of Marx and Lenin and with whom he discusses the Communist vision of a new social order. In time, he begins passing information to the Soviets at clandestine meetings in unoccupied Roman Catholic confessionals.

The CIA discovers Kirk's perfidy when the Soviets act on some bogus intelligence which Blackford deliberately feeds to their informant. Peregrine is then "eliminated" when he and Blackford fight a simulated air duel as part of a demonstration of competing American and British fighter jets. Over the closed-circuit radio by which they communicate, Oakes reveals his knowledge of his victim's espionage activities and gives Kirk an ultimatum: either crash his plane and die with reputation intact or risk exposure, disgrace, and almost certain execution. Peregrine chooses the former course and is given a hero's burial. At the Queen's insistence, the funeral eulogy is delivered by a grief-stricken Blackford Oakes.

Saving the Queen possesses many of the literary qualities which one might expect from a novel by Buckley. Among the most prominent of these is a puckish sense of humor. Indeed, supplementing the author's typically droll witticisms are some broad and bawdy knee-slappers. Consider, for example, this comment which his CIA colleague Anthony Trust makes to Blackford about midway through the novel: "I had lunch, just before coming over, with a State Department guy at a restaurant in Washington. McCarthy's going after the fags, as you know, and the department dropped about fifty people already this year. This guy said, 'McCarthy's got us so goddamn self-conscious, every time we buy a banana at the State Department cafeteria, we eat it like corn on the cob!'"[4]

Another amusing conversation takes place when, at a White House reception early in the novel, Blackford encounters the new president of Yale, Whitney Griswold. Griswold asks the young alumnus what he has been doing since graduation, and Oakes replies: "Well, among other things, I've just read Buckley's *God and Man at Yale.*" To which Griswold responds: "You must have a lot of time on your hands" (*S,* 57). (Buckley also manages—in Alfred Hitchcock fashion—to introduce himself into his other novels.)

Indeed, *Saving the Queen* is so clearly stamped with its author's personality that it seems like nothing so much as a virtuoso one-man performance: a monodrama starring William Buckley as William Buckley in many amusing but transparent disguises. One recalls that at the beginning of *Huckleberry Finn* Mark Twain lists the dialects which he is using so that his reader will not "suppose that all these characters were trying to talk alike and not succeeding." In the case of Buckley's novel, however, the characters do succeed in talking alike. Even Queen Caroline's vocabulary and syntax reveal a Buckleyan orotundity; a fact which causes her tryst with the author's alter-ego to assume a faintly auto-erotic quality.

It is this tryst, of course, which is the most notorious episode in *Saving the Queen.* It is also the first of what Buckley calls his obligatory sex scenes, bits of prurience inserted in his novels upon the advice of Vladimir Nabokov (who, incidentally, serves as the model for Dimitri Chadinoff, father of Blackford's nubile playmate in *Stained Glass*). Although there is a certain fantasy appeal in bedding the Queen of England, Buckley's rendering of that scene probably is not lurid enough ever to make the "Forum" section of *Penthouse* magazine. Indeed, the author himself has asserted that the only people he could imagine taking offense at such soft-core fare are the sort who read *National Review.*

Ultimately, Blackford's bedroom gymnastics force Buckley—on principle—to keep the novels in which they occur set in the 1950s. By the time of the Rockefeller Commission's investigation of the CIA in the mid-1970s (the ostensible time-present from which the bulk of *Saving the Queen* is an extended flashback), Oakes is married and has children. And Buckley has made it clear that he will not permit his hero any amorous conquests in transgression of the seventh commandment. (The operative principle here apparently is "fornication, sí; adultery, no.") Although it is true that his coupling with Queen Caroline—who is at least nominally a wife and mother—would appear to put Blackford in technical violation of this dictum, it is also true—as Emerson so sagely observed—that a foolish consistency is the hobgoblin of little minds.

The major subplot in *Saving the Queen* involves the harsh treatment which Blackford receives as an adolescent at the exclusive boy's school, Greyburn. A high-spirited young American—under the custody of his mother and British stepfather—Blackford is, by virtue of his instinctive iconoclasm and avowed isolationist politics, unpopular with the school's administration. One day he makes the fatal mistake of drawing on a classroom blackboard a picture of a particularly hated teacher: standing in academic gown, conjugating the Latin verb for "micturate," while performing the act itself. For this offense young Oakes receives a more severe birching than any that Stephen Dedalus suffered at the hands of the Jesuits. After administering this punishment, the headmaster gloats: *"Courtesy of Great Britain, sir."* But years later, a triumphant Blackford has the last laugh when, upon disengaging from his concupiscent service to the Queen, he proclaims: *"Courtesy of the United States, ma'am."* If on no other point, Buckley would seem to be in agreement with Eldridge Cleaver in regarding coitus as an essentially political act.

Hagiography

In *Stained Glass* Blackford's instructions are to neutralize Axel Wintergrin, an attractive young politican who—in hope of reunifying his homeland—is running for Chancellor of West Germany. Although such reunification would theoretically be in the best interests of the West, the architects of American foreign policy fear that Wintergrin's threat to Stalin could trigger a third world war. When covert efforts to undermine Axel's support prove futile, Blackford is teamed with the sensuous Russian spy Erika Chadinoff in a plot to assassinate the potential savior of the free world.

The conflict between Blackford's organizational loyalty and his affection for Axel gives *Stained Glass* a psychological tension which its predecesor lacks. "You had, in the case of *[Saving the]* Queen," Buckley notes in an interview, "somebody who felt no particular compunction, intellectually, against consummating a rather intricate operation. In *Stained Glass,* you have a protagonist torn because he becomes convinced that the rationale for an assassination he is asked to carry out is based on empirically false evidence, and . . . [because] he is asked to be an executioner of somebody he admires more than anybody he's ever met."[5]

Buckley's second novel may be more psychologically complex than his first, but it is no less entertaining. One recalls, for example, an encounter between Oakes and his stepfather's friend Lord Brougham. Although generally beloved, Lord Brougham had the habit—after his third drink of the evening—of describing his most recent day-long pheasant hunt with what the late Aristotle would have called perfect unity of time. "(*The Day Lord Brougham Shot the Pheasant,* by Jim Bishop, one survivor of an evening had suggested as an appropriate title and author for a book)."[6]

When Blackford finds himself the beneficiary of His Lordship's "narrative compulsion," our hero deftly handles the situation by putting his arm firmly on his tormentor's shoulder and saying in mock seriousness: "Lord Brougham, I'm too young to stand the suspense. Unless you shoot that bird in the next . . . sixty seconds, I'm going to have to ask the butler for some saltpeter" (*SG,* 39).

Although Buckley also pokes fun at himself by having his characters lampoon the depressingly ubiquitous media personality old Razzia, *Stained Glass* is ultimately conceived as neither drawing-room farce nor self-referential trope, but as high tragedy. Those forces which Buckley believes have insured the triumph of Communist interests in the post–World War II era—namely, Soviet villainy and Western impotence—finally converge to effect the martyrdom of a man who represents the best that Western civilization has to offer. Indeed, in the course of the novel, we find Axel Wintergrin increasingly assuming the role of secular saint.

In addition to being a courageous veteran of the anti-Nazi underground and the leading anti-Communist in Europe, Count Wintergrin is lord of Saint Anselm's—a vestigially feudal community built around a thirteenth-century chapel.[7] The damage done to that chapel by Allied bombing raids is being repaired under the supervision of young engineer Blackford Oakes. This job enables Oakes to infiltrate Wintergrin's camp and to orchestrate a lethal "accident" involving the chromoscope with which Axel examines stained glass for the chapel.

In the course of his labors, Blackford jokingly says to Axel: "If you would agree to get yourself martyred, I'm sure I could persuade Washington to *requisition* . . . your fingernails as relics for the altar at St. Anselm's" (*SG,* 143). But as the story progresses, Wintergrin's sanctity becomes less of a joke than a troublesome reality for Oakes. In fact, just before the count's actual martyrdom, his designated executioner reflects: "An Axel Wintergrin *could not be permitted to live* in this world" (*SG,* 296).

The young lord's death, in the very shadow of the Christian altar, may even have a kind of sacramental significance. "The chapel incarnates religion and technology," writes Ronald Berman, "which is to say that it holds together two great themes of Western culture. Wintergrin dies because a machine . . . has been designed not only to match modern and medieval stained glass but to explode through an electric charge. . . . Bill Buckley, like Henry Adams (who also knew about Gothic chapels), is writing about the Virgin and the Dynamo. The appalling literalness of the metaphor may be too much for coincidence."[8]

Finally, after Axel's death, Oakes is shown a note which the count had given to one of his trusted servants. The note informs that servant to report to "Herr Oakes," because "he may need help. . . . He will understand" (*SG*, 332). What Blackford understands is that Axel had seen through the plot against him, that he had willingly submitted to his fate, and that he had forgiven his murderers. "He was the finest man I ever knew," Blackford later says to Erika. "If there's anybody left like him, we must meet again to . . . eliminate him" (*SG*, 336; original ellipses).

The World Series of Espionage

By the time we get to *Who's On First,* it is the mid-1950s and the major Cold War conflict involves the Soviet-American race to put a satellite in orbit. Blackford's assignment is to kidnap Viktor Kapitsa, a Russian physicist attending a scientific conference in Paris—this being the International Geophysical Year—and to obtain valuable information about Soviet technology. As it turns out, Kapitsa is an incipient dissident who did time in Siberia during Stalin's regime. After cooperating fully with the CIA he is allowed to return, with an elaborate cover story, to his colleagues.

The dramatic tension heightens when the Soviet authorities see through Viktor's story and arrest him for espionage. In order to purchase Kapitsa's freedom, a Russian defector who is a close friend of Viktor's and who has worked with the CIA informs the Soviets of the location of an instrument which will provide them with the technological breakthrough necessary to launch Sputnik. The defector reveals what he has done in time for Blackford—should he decide to do so—to tip off the U.S. government. In effect, Oakes must choose between preserving America's lead in the space race and saving Kapitsa's life.

Of course, there were other conflicts of geopolitical significance transpiring in the mid-1950s. Nineteen-fifty-six, for example, was the year of the Hungarian revolution. And, as one might expect, Blackford is on hand doing his part to further the cause of human liberty. Indeed, the novel

128 WILLIAM F. BUCKLEY, JR.

opens with Oakes, standing at the window of his hotel room, witnessing the hanging of a Hungarian rebel named Theophilus Molnar.

Theo makes what "must have been a request, because the answer was unmistakably negative." Then:

> The assistant adjusted the noose around Theo's neck, and shouted out to the driver, and Blackford heard a gear engage. Whereupon, slowly, the hydraulic motor racing, the long arm of the portable crane began to rise, tugging up, slowly, the body of Theophilus Molnar, which, when his toes left the platform, began convulsively to thrash about, a whine of sorts issuing from the throat. . . . It required over three minutes before the twirling line hung down straight again, the boy's head bent over like the end of a shaggy black mop.[9]

Later, Oakes discovers what Theo had asked of the officer: "If he might be permitted to make the Sign of the Cross" (*W*, 10).

The Hungarian subplot reemerges when Molnar's fiancée Frieda and some friends kidnap Blackford in Paris. Thinking that he has betrayed their slain companion, they plot to kill Oakes in much the same way as Theo had died. At the last minute, however, their intended victim proves his innocence and exposes the real traitor—a Soviet spy who had been agitating strongly for Blackford's death. Back in her bedroom, Frieda demonstrates to her young American friend the depths of her remorse and the breadth of her gratitude.

What are probably the most entertaining sections of *Who's On First* involve conversations between CIA director Allen Dulles and former Secretary of State Dean Acheson. These men are close enough to Buckley's own mentality and temperament that he can put words in their mouths without striking an obviously false note. Their dialogue is clever, incisive, and articulate.

At one point Acheson quotes one of Buckley's favorite statements from John Stuart Mill: "'I never meant to say that Conservatives are generally stupid. I meant to say that stupid people are generally Conservative.'" (*W*, 12). And later, after the former secretary utters a mildly convoluted statement, Dulles remarks: "Jesus, Acheson, I bet you were insufferable even as a schoolboy." Without missing a beat, Acheson replies: "My first name is Dean, not Jesus; and the answer to your question is: I was" (*W*, 202).

In a provocative review of *Who's On First* Jack Chatfield notes that, like so many heroes in American literature, Blackford is—in Faulkner's phrase—"doomed to motion."[10] (By virtue of his restlessness, Oakes contrasts markedly with Sally Partridge—his long-suffering fiancée who supports Adlai Stevenson, writes essays on Jane Austen for the *Sewanee Review,* and generally keeps the home fires burning while our hero is abroad defending Western civilization and boffing more exotic young ladies: seductive British royalty, sultry KGB agents, tempestuous Hungarian freedom fighters, and assorted Parisian harlots.) Appropriately, Blackford's leisure reading on one predominantly personal jaunt to Sweden is Jack Kerouac's *On the Road.*

The title of Buckley's third novel alludes to the famous Abbott and Costello routine about a baseball squad which consists of players with names like "Who," "What," and "I don't know." Although the author's literal reference is to the Soviet-American competition to be first into space, one cannot help but think that by framing such a reference in terms of a nonsense comedy skit—part of which serves as an epigraph for *Who's On First*—Buckley is suggesting his own bemused contempt for that competition.[11]

Consider, for example, the novel's other epigraph—a quotation from Eric Hoffer, which reads in part: "On October 4, 1957, the Russians placed a medicine-ball-sized satellite in orbit. It needs an effort to remember how stunned we were when we discovered that the clodhopping Russians were technologically ahead of us, and that we would have to catch up with them. We reacted hysterically." The real tragedy of Sputnik had to do less with technology than with propaganda. With this single accomplishment, the Soviets did much to rehabilitate their image within the community of nations and to divert world attention from their genocidal invasion of Budapest. Because of the furor over space, the Theophilus Molnars of this world became obscure footnotes in the history of the fifties.[12]

U-2 Can Fly

The commercial success of Buckley's first three novels—putting him on the best-seller list for the first time since *McCarthy and His Enemies*—apparently has inspired their author to bless us with a succession of similar tales. If the highest art shuns formula (something which Faulkner criticized Hemingway's later work for failing to do), popular entertainments like the Blackford Oakes novels please precisely because they give us what we expect. *Marco Polo, If You Can* (1982) is no exception.

When we left our hero at the end of *Who's On First,* he had been separated from the CIA for valuing Viktor Kapitsa's life above America's supremacy in the space race. However, only the terminally naive would assume that Buckley had irretrievably consigned Blackford to the life of a civilian engineer. Even though Clint Eastwood threw away his badge—*á lá* Gary Cooper—at the end of *Dirty Harry,* he was back in action when the public demanded a sequel. So, too, is young Mr. Oakes available when the omnipotent Rufus (his CIA superior in the previous potboilers) concludes that truth, justice, and the American Way cannot survive without him.

The assignment this time around is to find the CIA mole who has been spiriting the minutes of National Security Council meetings to the Soviets. While that effort is going on, U.S. stategists fill the minutes with bogus information about American-Chinese cooperation in the U-2 spy flights. The idea is to exacerbate Sino-Soviet tensions, thus persuading the Russians to redeploy troops from the European to the Asian front. In order to string the Soviets along even further, Rufus decides that we need to allow them to capture an American spy plane bearing additional misinformation. The pilot of that plane is to be none other than Blackford Oakes.

By replacing Francis Gary Powers with his own fictional hero, Buckley does something that he has not done previously—he rewrites history. The notion that America would sacrifice one of its aircraft and risk the life of one of its agents in such a problematical scenario is only slightly less credible than the belief that the U-2 fiasco just happened. The statement from J. William Fulbright which provides the epigraph for *Marco Polo, If You Can* expresses sufficient skepticism concerning the latter thesis to make the former seem plausible. What Senator Fulbright cannot fathom is why, in the wake of Khrushchev's visit to the United States and his obvious desire to switch from military to economic competition, "the U-2 incident was allowed to take place." "No one will ever know," he concludes, "whether it was accidental or intentional."

The fourth Buckley novel is both shorter and more facile than its predecessors; however, familiar elements abound. Wit and humor are sprinkled throughout the book, with the most consistently hilarious scene depicting President Eisenhower's rage over the boorish behavior of Premier Khrushchev. Addressing the National Security Council, Eisenhower says:

"Any of you, any of you. I'm asking you a question: *Did you ever see Kroocheff drunk?*" . . . "Know what the son of a bitch told me last night? At *my* lodge? At *my* presidential retreat? Named after *my* grandson? Know what he said? He said—now, I quote him e-x-a-c-t-l-y.

"He said, 'Ike, you should watch your language.' *Called me 'Ike'!*" The President's eyes very nearly popped out.

The chief executive concludes by expressing his desire to walk up to Khrushchev, "eye to eye, then knee him one right in the crotch, then sit back and tell the interpreter to tell *'Nicky'* to watch *his* language."[13]

The obligatory sex scene in this novel joins Blackford with Amanda Gaither—a CIA clerk who also happens to be Dean Acheson's goddaughter. When it is discovered that Amanda is the mole who has been servicing the Soviets (she is an ideological as well as a physical nymphomaniac), Rufus asks Allen Dulles whether Acheson has said "he would never turn his back on Amanda Gaither?" (*MP*, 140). (The allusion to Acheson's defense of that earlier Soviet mole Alger Hiss is lost on a dull-witted J. Edgar Hoover.)

Once again, Blackford is sustained in his exploits by the image of his beloved Sally. (Although she may be given to feminist rhetoric, she possesses the patience and fidelity of Chaucer's Griselda.) And yet, having waited nearly a decade for her man to quit his rambling ways, she seems to represent something of a narrative problem for Buckley. We know, from *Saving the Queen,* that Blackford and Sally eventually tie the knot; however, as soon as that blessed union occurs, Buckley is committed to depriving his hero of the sexual license of a bachelor. The obvious solution, it seems to me, is to cast the obligatory fornications of the future Oakes novels in the form of flashbacks. (For example, "As Blackford gazed lovingly into Sally's eyes, he remembered that erotic Paris evening when he was putting it to the hot-blooded Emmanuelle.") Buckley could then conclude with a little homily on the superiority of *marital* bliss. The effect would be something like that of the sentimental comedies of the late Restoration and early eighteenth century: titillate the audience with illicit sex for four-and-a-half acts, then tack on a moralistic denouement. It is a sure-fire formula for success. As no less an authority than Dr. Johnson observed: "Colley Cibber was no blockhead."

The Moral of the Story

The Blackford Oakes novels are entertaining, intricately plotted, and stylishly written. As works of highbrow popular fiction, they are remarkably successful. Yet, from such a metaphysician as Buckley, one expects more. One expects, but fails to find, a serious exploration of the moral issues implicit in the stories he tells. Instead, the reader is offered some glib and sophomoric equivocation.

The one passage where Buckley comes closest to addressing the question of ethics occurs as Blackford embarks on his new career in *Saving the Queen:*

[H]e recalled an aphorism written on the blackboard by Mr. Simon: *Quod licet Jovi, non licet bovi.* . . . That which it is permitted for Jove to do is not necessarily permitted for a cow to do. We might in secure conscience lie and steal in order to secure the escape of human beings from misery or death; Stalin had no right to lie and steal in order to bring misery and death to others. Yet, viewed without paradigmatic moral coordinates, simpletons would say, simply: *Both sides lied and cheated*—a plague on both their houses (*S,* 146–47).

In a sense, Buckley's novels are anachronistic contributions to the genre of espionage fiction. "It was just as Britain lost its Empire," writes Robin W. Weeks, "lost its ability to blindly defend past principles, lost its position of world leadership, that the British spy novel turned from the heroics of a Richard Hannay or the moral certitudes of those who saw duty as all, to the moral gray areas of John Le Carre. The spy came in from the cold as those values that had held his predecessors in the cold were taken as hollow." Buckley, on the other hand, "wishes to take his readers back to the days before the waters had been muddied."[14]

Put simply, Blackford Oakes is a glorified hit man for whom the defeat of Communist objectives justifies the most unsavory of practices. One is troubled, for example, by the fact that Oakes dispatches Peregrine Kirk by inducing him to commit suicide (a ploy which the FBI once tried unsuccessfully against Martin Luther King). As an orthodox Roman Catholic, Buckley presumably regards suicide as a mortal sin; yet, Blackford seems to have no qualms about precipitating the commission of that sin. The pursuit of free-world geopolitical ends results in the loss not only of a human life, but of a human soul. Although Blackford does entertain reservations about the assassination of Axel Wintergrin—which he refuses to perform but allows to happen—and about the consignment of Viktor Kapitsa to the Gulag—which he prevents by withholding information from the CIA—those reservations are motivated less by abstract moral principle than by personal esteem for the men in question. (Since no comparable moral dilemma presents itself in *Marco Polo,* that novel simply avoids the issue altogether.) As Walter Goodman notes: "Our young agent's morale is excellent and his conscience is unspotted; clearly, this book was not written by a Catholic novelist."[15]

Although it would be grossly unfair to insist that Buckley write as well as Graham Greene, it is not too much to ask that he follow Greene's example in confronting the moral conundrums in fiction with an attitude of total seriousness. (One need only compare Greene's recent espionage novel *The Human Factor* [1978] with any of the Oakes books to see what I mean.) What is most vexing about Buckley's otherwise engaging thrillers is not so much the ideology they espouse as the smugness with which they ignore ethical ambiguity. "I may have my faults," the late Jimmy Hoffa once said, "but being wrong ain't one of them."

Chapter Fourteen

A Benediction

In his introduction to *Rumbles Left and Right,* Russell Kirk reminds us of T. S. Eliot's observation that "there are no lost causes, because there are no gained causes" (*R, 9*). Although such an epigram can sustain one in times of adversity, it should also serve as a chastening reminder that all glory is fleeting. The seeming triumph of *National Review* conservatism in the 1980 elections poses challenges to Buckley and company of the sort that they never faced while on the outside looking in.

If the conservative movement is stronger today than it was when *National Review* was founded in 1955, it is because the status quo is itself more liberal. Since it is difficult to attack convincingly a system with which one is in fundamental agreement, schematic conservatives of the fifties were reduced to such extreme ploys as denouncing Eisenhower for his leftist sympathies and canonizing Joe McCarthy. What program they had seemed to be little more than a brief for reversing the then popular welfare reforms of the Roosevelt and Truman years. And with cold-war liberals preaching the doctrine of containment, anti-Communism was not even an exclusively conservative issue.

How different things were by 1980! The upheavals of the sixties had created a genuine nostalgia for quieter times, and the social experimentation of federal bureaucrats had provoked a backlash against big government. Also, during the seventies the country had reached the point where a substantial majority of the voting-age population had no vivid memories of the Great Depression. Liberalism had been transformed from a purr word to a snarl word, and for the first time in memory all the intellectual innovation seemed to be on the right. (Indeed, had it not been for Watergate, the conservative renaissance might have coincided with our Bicentennial rather than coming four years later.)

Like many dissident movements, however, conservatism was internally most coherent when times were bad for it and most fragmented when the time came to take power. In a February 2, 1981 feature entitled "The

134

Right: A House Divided?" *Newsweek* identified at least five different groups in the Reagan coalition: the Old Right, the New Right, the Religious Right, Neo-conservatives, and the GOP Establishment. While each of these groups undoubtedly exists, it seems to me that the profusion of terminology obscures rather than elucidates the actual layout of the political landscape. Thus, it might be helpful to go back to the old tripartite division of the fifties and see what has happened to economic libertarians, anti-Communists, and cultural traditionalists.[1]

If there was one thing that right-wing economists could always agree on, it was that deficit spending was based on the dangerous chimera of a free lunch and that eliminating or at least holding the line on this hazardous practice was an economic, perhaps even a moral, imperative. How exactly to do this has proved a somewhat more vexing problem. Those who call themselves monetarists argue for tight money and immediately lower deficits as a brake against inflation. Their supply-side brethren are equally convinced that the economic stimulus provided by loose money and massive tax cuts will so prime the economic pump that prosperity and balanced budgets will be just around the corner. The only way to satisfy both groups would be to make drastic cuts in federal spending. Unfortunately, this cannot be done without pruning the military budget (and thus running afoul of anti-Communist sentiment) or reducing increases in middle-class entitlements (and thus antagonizing the Silent Majority). The only politically expedient course of action is to slash away at the social safety net—a policy which hurts the most destitute without having other than symbolic impact on budget deficits.

Persons of the anti-Communist persuasion must regard the fifties as a Golden Age and everything since as a slow boat to Munich. The nuclear ante has been raised to the point where containment is now the only game in town. Ironically, the group which has remained most faithful to the anti-Soviet crusade consists not of old-time conservatives but of Cold-War liberals who refused to adopt the isolationist line of the post-Vietnam left. These people—Norman Podhoretz, Irving Kristol, Daniel Patrick Moynihan et al.—are now somewhat confusingly labeled as "neo-conservative."[2] They are perhaps best understood, however, as fairly traditional social democrats. This lineage makes them considerably more militant than those Chamber of Commerce types who are loathe to impose any kind of economic sanctions on the Soviets. Not being blinded by free-market pieties, these social democrats are able to remind the antisanction crowd of Lenin's statement that when the last of the bourgeois is hanged, a capitalist will sell the hangman the rope.

In recent years, the most action on the right has probably been in the traditionalist camp. For purposes of clarity, we can further divide this camp into high-rent and low-rent traditionalists. The high-rent faction consists of cultural elitists who are intent on defending Western Civilization against the evils of relativism, secularism, and egalitarianism. Their work can be found in the pages of *Modern Age, Chronicles of Culture,* the *New Oxford Review,* and the "Books, Arts, and Manners" section of *National Review.* Politically, the most prominent spokesman for the high-rent traditionalists is George F. Will. In thoughtful and superbly crafted essays, Will regularly applies the principles of Edmund Burke to everything from international relations to the American League's Designated Hitter Rule.

Among the low-rent traditionalists, we can include those who are generally termed the "New Right." To be scrupulously accurate, however, this group is neither new nor right. It is at least as old as the Know-Nothing movement of the early nineteenth century and is less conservative than populist in orientation. Major figures in this subcoalition include fundamentalist Protestants like Jerry Falwell, profamily Catholics like Phyllis Schlafly, and mail-order technicians like Richard Viguerie. Eschewing the libertarian passion for limited government, these people represent what Garry Wills so aptly characterizes as "apple-pie authoritarianism."

It should not be supposed that these categories are either airtight or mutually exclusive. Rather, they are protean aggregations which are capable of coming together in ad-hoc coalitions around specific issues and individual candidates (for example, the Reagan campaign). It is thus possible to place someone like Buckley in more than one category without suggesting that in his ecumenical zeal he is trying to be all things to all conservatives.

In terms of economic policy, Buckley has always been a free marketeer who distrusted the welfare leviathan and the budget deficits on which it fed. (Strategically, he and *National Review* have recently cast their lot with the supply-siders against the monetarists.) Nevertheless, he shares the neo-conservatives' willingness to subordinate the purity of the marketplace to the struggle against Communism. In Buckley's utopia, however, one suspects that the interests of the free market and larger geopolitical concerns would never be in conflict.

By disposition, Buckley is probably most at home among the high-rent traditionalists. His pre–Vatican II religious sympathies, his love for Bach, and his general disdain for the masses suggest that in today's world he considers snobbery to be something of an heroic virtue. However, these traits also tend to impede visceral identification between Buckley and the redneck constituency of the "New Right." Even though they may admire him, these people are apt to think Buckley a blue-blood preppy who is far too soft on dope, smut, and perversion. And yet, both he and the neo-populist right share the philosophical patrimony of Willmoore Kendall.

As interesting as Buckley's ideological gyrations may be for the political scientist and the historian of ideas. he must finally be judged as a man of letters. In this regard, it is perhaps best to view him as what Mitchell S. Ross calls a "literary politician," one who has chosen "to practice politics by writing books."[3] Of such a figure, Ross observes: "His writings both mark and redirect the shifting political winds. The work of a literary politician joins personal experience to political occurrence; it is likely to be full of surprises. His task is that act of public education so often wrongly listed among the duties of the professional politician. The purpose of the professional politician is to gain and maintain office; the purpose of the literary politician is to explain the people to the people. This makes him one of the most powerful unanointed officials of the Republic."[4]

Although it is no more possible to separate Buckley from his works than it is the dancer from the dance, it is possible to distinguish between his better artifacts and those which are less successful. To do this, it is perhaps helpful to divide his literary corpus into four distinct genres: anthologies, novels, idea books, and autobiographical works. Each has its specific virtues and its endemic defects.

The six Buckley anthologies are each so mixed in quality that it is difficult to rank one ahead of the others. The only one which seems in any way distinctive is *Rumbles Left and Right* (1963), and that is because it consists entirely of pieces which predate its author's newspaper column. What we find in *The Jeweler's Eye* (1968), *The Governor Listeth* (1970), *Inveighing We Will Go* (1972), *Execution Eve* (1975), and *A Hymnal* (1978) are several fine essays scattered among essentially topical columns. Although some of these columns are quite good, the constraints of writing against a thrice-weekly deadline produce varied results. Moreover, when a goodly number of short pieces are brought together, it is hard to avoid the appearance of superficiality.

As a novelist, Buckley is fun without being aesthetically or philosophically profound. The best of the Blackford Oakes tales is probably *Stained Glass* (1978). It possesses the virtues of the other novels as well as a symbolic resonance which the others lack. *Who's On First* (1980) is worth reading for the Dulles-Acheson dialogues, while *Saving the Queen* (1976) has the ingenuous charm of a beginner's effort. *Marco Polo* (1982), however, offers little beyond the novelty of its thesis.

If Buckley's fiction provides more sweetness than light, his idea books do just the opposite. *God and Man at Yale* (1951) and *McCarthy and His Enemies* (1954) are turgid early works which are of more historical than literary interest, while his most recent venture in the genre—*Four Reforms* (1973)—is mostly a feast for position-paper junkies. *Up From Liberalism* (1959) is thus the most stylistically distinguished of Buckley's idea books. It is analytical, urbane, and thoroughly engaging. Although it may appear old hat today, it must have been quite impressive in an age when intellectual pronouncements from a conservative seemed about as oxymoronic as Gomer Pyle's singing Grand Opera.

To my mind, Buckley is at his best when he is writing about himself. The affability, personal grace, and self-deprecatory humor which his intimates find so endearing are all there in his autobiographical works. And yet, even here, objections can be raised. Although *Airborne* (1976) seems to be everybody's favorite, it finally appeals to those whose interest in sailing is greater than my own. *United Nations Journal* (1974) is good, but it is perhaps too accurate an account of the U.N. to sustain one's interest over a full-length book. *Cruising Speed* (1971) also tends to wear a bit thin. The diary of a typical and not particularly momentous week in the life of its author, it is likely to strike all but the most die-hard Buckley fan as an account of *The Week Lord Brougham Shot the Pheasant*.

Surely, Buckley's best book overall is *The Unmaking of a Mayor* (1966). To begin with, as pure memoir it ranks among its author's most interesting and amusing autobiographical narratives. In addition, its substantive proposals display the intellectual originality of *Four Reforms,* and its attacks on John Lindsay the analytical rigor of *Up From Liberalism.* Thus, his single foray into electoral politics gives Buckley a coherent framework for showcasing some of his finest writing.[5]

But here, perhaps I am indulging a personal preference. At the time I read *The Unmaking of a Mayor,* Bill Buckley seemed to me a magical figure. One of my prized possessions was a poster from his campaign—it brightened several dorm rooms and apartments until it was lost in one of many moves. Perhaps some of my early fascination with the campaigner was lost with it. Still, *The Unmaking of a Mayor* was *The Catcher in the Rye* of my undergraduate years.

It is generally acknowledged that discussing a living writer— particularly a prolific one—is sort of like shooting at a moving target.

Nevertheless, Bill Buckley's longevity and impact almost require us to venture some generalizations about his literary accomplishment to date. It seems to me that, even beyond winning converts to his point of view, Buckley will be remembered for having brought to political journalism an almost sensuous love of the English language and a much needed sense of humor. Indeed, the style and wit which distinguish him from the somber moralists who inhabit so much of the political landscape finally amount to more than a mere difference of tone. "Laughter is the mode that refuses to take the world quite that seriously," writes Jeffrey Hart:

> Recognizing the inherent contradictions and absurdities of man's existence, it steps back and allows the world to *be* the world. Thus, Kierkegaard could say profoundly that the earnestness of one's faith is tested by one's "sensitivity to the comical"; and Malraux, writing on the history of art, could take the appearance of the "archaic smile" in sculpture as a sign that man had become aware of his soul. Serious as they are about politics, the conservatives who write for *National Review* do not seem to consider it the ultimate category; and humor, as they employ it, is the sign of a proper distance—of temporary removal; of the willingness to step back, and, in the higher sense of the word, play with the subject at hand.[6]

The facetious claims of *National Review* notwithstanding, the election of Ronald Reagan did not make Bill Buckley into an establishment mouthpiece, nor did it cause him to lose his sense of humor. Inveterate gadflies are rarely pacified by such a paltry thing as success. "You may be the new sheriff in town," Mort Sahl told Jack Kennedy, "but I'm still an outlaw."

Notes and References

Chapter One

1. Quoted in Buckley's *The Unmaking of a Mayor* (New York: Bantam Books, 1967), pp. 367–68; hereafter cited in the text as *U*.
2. *National Review,* November 28, 1980, p. 1434.
3. Dan Wakefield, "William F. Buckley, Jr.: Portrait of a Complainer," *Esquire,* January 1961, p. 50.
4. It should be pointed out that the Buckley family heritage is neither as Irish nor as Catholic as that of the Kennedys. Bill Buckley's mother has no Irish blood (she is of French, Swiss, and German extraction) and one of his father's grandparents was Protestant.
5. L. Clayton Dubois, "The First Family of Conservatism," *New York Times Magazine,* August 9, 1970, p. 11.
6. Larry L. King, "God, Man, and William F. Buckley," *Harper's,* March 1967, p. 55.
7. See *W.F.B.—An Appreciation,* ed. William F. Buckley, Jr. and Priscilla L. Buckley (New York, 1959), pp. 243–44.
8. Garry Wills, *Confessions of a Conservative* (Garden City, N.Y., 1979), pp. 14–15.
9. Ibid., p. 21.
10. Ibid., p. 18.
11. If Bill inherited his combativeness from his father, he might well have derived his gentler qualities from his mother. Commenting on Mrs. Buckley, Susan Sheehan writes: "To her, Bill isn't great because his column appears in 315 newspapers, but because when he saw a *National Review* employee in tears over the fact that the mortgage on her parents' home was about to be foreclosed, he wrote out a blank check and handed it to her; because when her daughter Aloise was stricken with a cerebral hemorrhage, Bill flew to Camden to break the bad news more gently to their mother than he could have done over the telephone; and because when one of Bill's childhood nurses thought she was dying and didn't want to die without seeing her former charge, he canceled all his engagements and flew to Mexico to her bedside." ("The Battling Buckley Women," *McCall's,* October 1971, p. 156)
12. Charles Lam Markmann, *The Buckleys: A Family Examined* (New York, 1973), p. 73.
13. Wills, *Confessions,* pp. 15–16.

14. Garry Wills, "Buckley, Buckley, Bow Wow Wow," *Esquire,* January 1968, p. 158.

15. *Cruising Speed* (New York, 1971), p. 222; hereafter cited in the text as *CS.*

16. Wills, "Buckley, Buckley," p. 76.

17. Ibid., p. 155.

18. Wills, *Confessions,* pp. 10–11.

19. *Commentary,* April 1956, pp. 367–73.

20. Ibid., p. 367.

21. Ibid., p. 368.

22. *A Hymnal* (New York, 1978), p. 404; hereafter cited in the text as *H.*

23. Markmann, *The Buckleys,* p. 86.

24. King, "God, Man," p. 53.

25. *Stained Glass* (New York: Warner Books, 1979), p. 109.

26. King, "God, Man," p. 53.

27. *The Jeweler's Eye* (New York: Berkley Medallion, 1969), p. 264; hereafter cited in the text as *JE.*

28. Buckley's tolerance of off-color comments and double entendres occasionally gets him into trouble with the more straitlaced types at *National Review.* Indeed, there was a veritable outbreak of Mrs. Grundyism on the *NR* staff when, in the process of making a purely linguistic point, their editor noted that a man walking up to a British Ms. who held a kitten on her lap could—with perfect impunity—ask to "stroke her pussy"; whereas, he would be likely to get his face slapped for similarly accosting an American lass. See *Execution Eve* (New York, 1975), pp. 343–48 hereafter cited in the text as *EE.*

29. *National Review,* December 31, 1980, p. 1645.

Chapter Two

1. "Notes Toward an Empirical Definition of Conservatism," in *The Jeweler's Eye,* p. 11.

2. See Nash's *The Conservative Intellectual Movement in America Since 1945* (New York, 1976).

3. After a debate with Buckley on "The Real Meaning of the Right Wing in America," Norman Mailer suggested that the implicit thesis of Buckley's position was that "the nature of the Right Wing is to attack figures on the Left" (*The Presidential Papers* [New York: Berkley Medallion, 1970], p. 174).

4. In 1945, Hayek became an election issue in England "when Clement Attlee accused the Conservative Party of adopting the Austrian economist's allegedly reactionary principles" (Nash, *Conservative,* p. 6). In America, the *"Reader's Digest* eagerly condensed the book for its readers and arranged for the Book-of-the-Month Club to distribute more than a million reprints" (ibid., p. 7). For Buckley's views on Hayek and *The Road to Serfdom,* see *Essays on Hayek,* ed. Fritz Machlup (New York, 1976), pp. 95–106.

5. Founded by Albert Jay Nock in the 1920s, the *Freeman* underwent many transformations. Chamberlain, Hazlitt, and Chodorov all edited the journal at various times during the thirties and forties.

6. It is true that Kirk's *The Conservative Mind* discusses several New England thinkers (Hawthorne, Brownson, the Adamses; More, Santayana, and Babbitt). However, these Yankees were considerably less representative of their region than their counterparts were of the South.

7. Nash, *Conservative,* p. 237.

8. In *God and Man at Yale,* Buckley attacks the epistemological optimism which underlies a belief in absolute majority rule. We cannot permit a marketplace of ideas, he argues, because the people might choose to follow a Hitler or a Stalin. However, if the marketplace of ideas is to be closed, someone has to do the closing. In a democratic society, that task is performed by representative institutions which reflect—however imperfectly—the will of the majority. Though Buckley is careful to keep the mob from being subverted by his opponents, he is not above using it to guard his own most cherished values.

9. After the apostles James and John, who were known as the "Sons of Thunder." See Mark 3:17 (KJV).

10. *Up From Liberalism* (New York, 1959), p. 114; hereafter cited in the text as *UL.*

11. Nash, *Conservative,* p. 177.

12. In *Did You Ever See a Dream Walking,* ed. Buckley (Indianapolis, 1970), pp. 3–37.

13. Ibid., pp. 20–21.

Chapter Three

1. Originally published in *Playboy,* this interview is the initial entry in *Inveighing We Will Go* (New York, 1972), p. 19; hereafter cited in the text as *I.*

2. *McCarthy and His Enemies* (Chicago, 1954), p. 335.

3. Nash, *Conservative,* p. 114.

4. Ibid., p. 112. Speaking of *McCarthy and His Enemies,* Mitchell S. Ross observes: "It is possible that this genuflection before the Wisconsin Savonarola sacrificed a generation of would-be *National Review* conservatives in the academies" (*The Literary Politicians* [Garden City, N.Y., 1978], p. 19).

5. Here, Buckley is quoting from Murray Kempton's account of the Kutcher story. See *A Hymnal,* p. 149.

6. *Rumbles Left and Right* (New York: Mcfadden, 1964), p. 35. Hereafter cited in the text as *R.*

7. See James Joyce's *Ulysses* (New York: Random House, 1961), p. xii. The text of Judge Woolsey's decision lifting the U.S. ban on Joyce's novel is contained in the front matter of this edition.

8. Such a position is articulated by Buckley in *The Jeweler's Eye,* pp. 109–11.

9. This quotation comes from a speech which Buckley delivered before the Philadelphia Society and which was excerpted in the *Wall Street Journal,* May 21, 1982.

Chapter Four

1. Steve Allen made this point in a 1963 debate with Buckley. See *Dialogues in Americanism* (Chicago, 1964), p. 52.

2. Buckley thinks that we should have a national commission which would make annual objective reports about the condition of human rights in the various countries of the world. There would be no necessary correlation, however, between the findings of this commission and American foreign policy. See Buckley's "Human Rights and Foreign Policy: A Proposal," *Foreign Affairs* 58 (Spring 1980), 775–96.

3. *The Governor Listeth* (New York: Berkley Medallion, 1970), p. 269. Hereafter cited in the text as *GL.*

4. Quoted in Buckley's *United Nations Journal: A Delegate's Odyssey* (New York, 1974), p. 14; hereafter cited in the text as *UN.*

5. Ward Sinclair of the *Washington Post* seized upon this statement as evidence that Buckley finally was wrong about something. Balboa, not Cortez, was the discoverer of the Pacific Ocean. Chairman Bill, however, had the last word. "The lines are from John Keats," he writes to the editor of the *Post.* "His sonnet 'On First Looking into Chapman's Homer.' I felt presumptuous enough correcting Ronald Reagan's foreign policy without straightening out Keats's historical solecism. But tell Mr. Sinclair not to worry: it happens all the time, people's inability to tell where I leave off and Keats begins." See "Notes and Asides," *National Review,* February 3, 1978, p. 141.

6. Ibid.

Chapter Five

1. According to legend, when Yogi Berra was once asked if he wanted his pizza cut into four pieces or eight, he replied: "Four. I don't think I could eat eight." Much liberal economic thought is based on approximately the opposite fallacy.

2. In his essay on Hayek, Buckley comments on *"the moral inferiority of capitalists" (Essays on Hayek,* p. 100). What he has in mind are businessmen who sell police technology to the Soviets and who advertise in left-wing and pornographic magazines. He remains silent, however, on the moral implications of such things as consumer fraud and environmental pollution.

3. In *The Literary Politicians,* Mitchell S. Ross notes that *Up From Liberalism's* critique of method obsession "would stand as doctrine for some

time, only to be expunged in 1973 with the publication of Buckley's *Four Reforms*" (p. 30).

4. *Four Reforms* (New York: Berkley Medallion, 1975), p. 65. Unless otherwise noted, all figures cited are Buckley's. Hereafter this book will be cited in the text as *FR*.

5. One of the imponderables of supply-side tax-cut theory, however, is uncertainty about whether the rich will use their newly augmented incomes for savings and investment or for inflationary consumption.

6. The left-leaning but independent-minded economist Lester C. Thurow points out that consumption taxes, if combined with tax credits, can be made non-regressive. In 1980, he writes, "a 10 percent value-added tax with a $1,000-per-household income-tax credit would have raised $153 billion" ("Saving Social Security," *Newsweek,* October 26, 1981, p. 71). It would seem to make more sense from both a populist and a supply-side standpoint to tax the consumption rather than the income of the wealthy.

Chapter Six

1. Unlike many advocates of preferential hiring, Buckley voices some concern for the rights of those sacrificed on the altar of historic reparation. The case for racial preference, he points out, "needs to be carefully made and understood primarily for the reason that those who tend to make it tend to be immune from the practical consequences of it" (*Governor,* p. 165).

2. Wills, *Confessions,* pp. 76–77.

3. In fact, if the situation is viewed in purely quantitative terms, one could argue for the revival of scapegoating. As C. S. Lewis, who was certainly no liberal, observed: "If the justification of exemplary punishment is not to be based on desert but solely on its efficiency as a deterrent, it is not absolutely necessary that the man we punish should even have committed the crime. . . . When a victim is urgently needed for exemplary purposes and a guilty victim cannot be found, all the purposes of deterrence will be equally served by the punishment (call it 'cure' if you prefer) of an innocent victim, provided that the public can be cheated into thinking him guilty" (*God in the Dock* [Grand Rapids, Mich.: Eerdmans, 1970], p. 291).

4. Buckley himself makes much the same point in arguing against excessive measures for achieving racial integration. "There would be less speeding," he writes, "and hence less violent slaughter—the two figures, the experts inform us, are inextricably related—if speeders were packed off to jail for a week. Even so, notwithstanding the established correlation between fast driving and aborted lives, we shrink from so drastic a penalty" (*Rumbles,* p. 93).

5. See *Execution Eve,* pp. 391–400, for Buckley's discussion of this issue.

6. This point is made by Buckley in a discussion of Colson's efforts on behalf of prison reform. See *National Review,* May 14, 1982, p. 585.

Chapter Seven

1. See *Running Against the Machine,* ed. Peter Manso (Garden City, N.Y.: Doubleday, 1968), p. 112.

2. Indeed, Baker himself notes: "William F. Buckley, Jr., another man of letters, faced the same handicap [as Mailer] in his mayoralty campaign four years ago" (Ibid.).

3. "[A]lthough he was a firebrand tory, utterly opposed to the New Deal," Barton "was uproariously popular, even while pledging to devote himself to the repeal of one obsolete law each week, and firmly opposing entry into the Second World War. He was, indeed, *the* Barton of Roosevelt's 'Martin, Barton, and Fish,' the big political anti-doxology of the late thirties" (*Unmaking of a Mayor,* p. 71). Barton also wrote *The Man Nobody Knows,* a book which admiringly depicts Jesus Christ as a first-century precursor to today's high-powered advertising agents.

4. Consider, for example, Lincoln's famous homily: "You cannot bring prosperity by discouraging thrift. You cannot strengthen the weak by weakening the strong. You cannot help the poor by destroying the rich. You cannot establish sound security on borrowed money. You cannot keep out of trouble by spending more than you earn. You cannot build character and courage by taking away man's initiative and independence. You cannot help men permanently by doing for them what they can and should do for themselves" (quoted in *Unmaking of a Mayor,* p. 87).

5. "Politics and the English Language," in *The Collected Essays, Journalism and Letters of George Orwell,* ed. Sonia Orwell and Ian Argus (New York: Harcourt Brace and World, 1968), 4:139.

6. Button, *Lindsay: A Man for Tommorrow* (New York: Random House, 1965), p. 23; quoted in *Unmaking of a Mayor,* p. 90.

7. Commenting on *his* candidate, Norman Mailer's campaign manager Joe Flaherty writes: "The things I cherished in Mailer as a writer—his daring, his unpredictability, his gambling, and his bluffing—were the very things that made me want to strangle him as a politician" (Joe Flaherty, *Managing Mailer* [New York: Berkley Medallion, 1971], p. 183).

8. See John Leo, "Very Dark Horse in New York," *New York Times Magazine,* September 5, 1965, p. 9.

9. See "Sniper," *Time,* November 3, 1967, p. 71.

10. Flaherty, *Managing Mailer,* p. 191.

11. When one adds the votes which George Wallace received to Nixon's total, the defeat of liberalism's standard-bearer Hubert Humphrey seems all the more devastating.

12. In the general election that year Marchi finished third, behind Lindsay (who had secured a place on the ballot by once again winning the Liberal Party's endorsement) and right-wing Democrat Mario Procaccino. Although it is not

clear that Buckley's presence in the 1965 race threw that election to Lindsay, it is likely that Marchi's candidacy had precisely that effect in 1969. Most obviously, he won conservative votes that otherwise would have gone to Procaccino. Also, by depriving Lindsay of the Republican nomination, Marchi made it easier for liberal Democrats and independents to vote for the mayor.

Had the Democrats nominated a liberal, however, Marchi (or Buckley) would have stood an excellent chance of winning a plurality in the general election. Conventional wisdom holds that the surprise nomination of Procaccino was due to a fragmentation of the Democratic left among three candidates: Herman Badillo, James Scheuer, and Norman Mailer. Since Badillo's margin of defeat was less than the total vote which Mailer received, many hold Mailer responsible for Procaccino's nomination and, ultimately, Lindsay's reelection.

Chapter Eight

1. King, "God, Man," p. 55.

2. For a learned discussion of this phenomenon by a man of liberal credentials, see Raoul Berger's *Government by Judiciary: The Transformation of the Fourteenth Amendment* (Cambridge: Harvard University Press, 1977).

3. See Michael Schwartz, "A Break for Poor Parents," *National Review,* August 7, 1981, pp. 900–902.

4. The money equivalent of a child's right to a public education, capable of being cashed in as part payment toward private schooling.

5. "Blacks, who make up just 2 per cent of the total Catholic population, now account for almost 8 per cent of the Catholic school enrollment" (Schwartz, "A Break," p. 901).

6. Max Eastman, "Buckley Versus Yale," *American Mercury,* December 1951, p. 23.

7. *God and Man at Yale* (Chicago, 1951); hereafter cited in the text as *GM*.

8. For a particularly virulent response to Buckley, see McGeorge Bundy, "The Attack on Yale," *Atlantic Monthly,* November 1951, pp. 50–52.

9. See "God and Man at Yale: Twenty-five Years Later," in *A Hymnal,* p. 424. And yet, Buckley also has said "I think people are a bore who create a theology around private enterprise." See "Sniper," *Time,* November 3, 1967, p. 78.

10. Herbert Marcuse, "Repressive Tolerance," in *A Critique of Pure Tolerance* (Boston: Beacon Press, 1969), p. 88.

11. Robert Paul Wolff, *The Ideal of the University* (Boston: Beacon Press, 1969), p. 70.

12. Ibid., p. 73.

13. Describing the modern university in a passage which could have come straight out of *God and Man at Yale,* Wolff writes: "The universities at present are sanctuaries for social critics who would find it very hard to gain a living

elsewhere in society. Who but a university these days would hire Herbert Marcuse, Eugene Genovese, or Barrington Moore, Jr.? Where else are anarchists, socialists, and followers of other unpopular persuasions accorded titles, honors, and the absolute security of academic tenure? . . . How majestic and unassailable is the university president who protects his dissident faculty with an appeal to the sanctity of academic freedom!" (Ibid., p. 75).

Chapter Nine

1. See Garry Wills, *Politics and Catholic Freedom* (Chicago, 1964), pp. 3, 4. Unless otherwise noted, references to the *Mater et Magistra* controversy come from this source. Incidentally, it was Wills, not Buckley, who came up with the "Mater, si; Magistra, no" quip. At this time, the public still remembered Castro's slogan: "Cuba, si; Yanqui, no."
2. Ibid., p. 5.
3. Ibid.
4. Ibid., pp. 13–14.
5. Wills, *Confessions,* p. 63.
6. Ibid.
7. Quoted in ibid, pp. 63–64. One is reminded of the words of that earlier Catholic polemicist Alexander Pope: "Yes I am proud. I must be proud to see / Men not afraid of God afraid of me" ("Epilogue to the Satires," 11. 208–9).
8. Seabury, "Trendier Than Thou," *Harper's,* October 1978, pp. 39–40, 42–43, 46–47, 50, 52. Although Seabury's specific target is the Episcopal Church, his comments could apply with equal force to recent developments within the Roman Communion.
9. See *Spectrum of Catholic Attitudes,* ed. Robert Campbell, O.P. (Milwaukee, 1969), for Buckley's comments on a wide range of religious issues.
10. The solution which was finally arrived at in the American church was to authorize a book with alternative liturgies—both traditional and modern. This "compromise," like the proverbial camel, resembles a horse designed by a committee.
11. In *The Jeweler's Eye,* Buckley writes: "The reason why Christian conservatives can associate with atheists is that we hold that, above all, faith is a gift and that, therefore, there is no accounting for the bad fortune that has beset those who do not believe or the good fortune that has befallen those who do" (p. 24).

Chapter Ten

1. See L. Clayton Dubois, "The First Family of Conservatism," *New York Times Magazine,* August 9, 1970, p. 28.
2. This and other excerpts from Chambers's letters to Buckley can be found in "The Last Years of Whittaker Chambers," in *Rumbles,* pp. 144–63. For a

considerably larger selection, see *Odyssey of a Friend: Whittaker Chambers' Letters to William F. Buckley, Jr.* (New York, 1969).

3. Markmann, *The Buckleys,* p. 109.

4. The employees of Goldwater's department store "earn more than their competitors, and yet they work a 37-hour week, and enjoy fringe benefits ranging from an employees' swimming pool to a retirement fund" (*R,* 26).

Chapter Eleven

1. *Airborne: A Sentimental Journey* (New York, 1976), p. 15; hereafter cited in the text as *A.*

2. In *Confessions of a Conservative,* Garry Wills tells us of getting "a telephone call from Bill: 'Do you know of a person named Joe Nu-*math*?' You mean Joe *Nay*-muth? 'Is that how you pronounce it? Well, Harold Hayes of *Esquire* has asked me to do a piece on him. Is there enough to bother?' I said I thought so; he could tell when he met him. 'Oh, I don't have time to *meet* him'" (p.13).

3. See "Strange Bedfellows," in *Execution Eve,* pp. 237–44.

4. Actually the specific reference here is to a *New Yorker* condensation of *Airborne.* The exception that proves the rule is a Dr. Louis E. Prickman, who writes to Buckley: "*Airborne* is totally without merit, except for its title which, although clever, is a misnomer, since a substantial part of the trip was under power, with barrels of fuel lashed on deck, no less. The book has no substance, no message, no entertainment, no value. Your publisher should be more discriminating." To which Buckley replies: "Dear Doc: Please call me Bill. Can I call you by your nickname? / Cordially, / WFB" (*H,* 379–80). Since the publication of *Airborne,* Buckley has come out with yet another sailing memoir: *Atlantic High* (New York, 1982). Unfortunately, this book was published too recently to be considered in the present study.

5. Upon meeting John Wayne, Joan Didion realized that the actor's face "was in certain ways more familiar than my husband's" (*Slouching Towards Bethlehem* [New York: Farrar, Straus and Giroux, 1968], p. 41).

6. The closest thing we get to lyricism is Hugh Kenner's elegy upon the sinking of Buckley's first yacht *The Panic:* "She had done much for her friends, in the summers before her side was stove in. She had taken them all around the Sound, and along the New England coast, and even to Bermuda (thrice), and shown them Wood's Hole, and the Great Fish that eats taffrail logs, and the Kraken, and the strange men of Onset with their long faces, and perfect Edgartown; and lapsed them at night gently to rest; and given them the wind and sun and often more rain than they knew how to be comfortable in; and made for them a place of adventure and refreshment and peace; and taught them this, that beyond illusion it is possible to be for hours and days on end perfectly and inexpressibly happy" (*A,* 8–9).

Chapter Twelve

1. Kilpatrick made this point in his syndicated column "The Writer's Art." I read it in the *Columbus Dispatch,* May 30, 1982, p. H7.
2. Ross, *Literary Politicians,* p. 14.
3. Joan Didion, *The White Album* (New York: Simon and Schuster, 1979), pp. 126–27.
4. Quoted in *Newsweek,* September 20, 1965, p. 29. About a year later, Buckley told Larry L. King: "When I sent Norman Mailer a copy of my latest book [*The Unmaking of a Mayor*] I turned over to the index in the back and wrote 'Hi!' by his name. Knowing Mailer, he'll immediately go to the index to evaluate his own role, and that 'Hi!' will just kill him!" (King, "God, Man," p. 56).
5. The Dickens reference is Cavett's.
6. Markmann, *The Buckleys,* pp. 272–73.
7. See Buckley's "On Experiencing Gore Vidal," in *Smiling Through the Apocalypse,* ed. Harold Hayes (New York: Dell, 1969), p. 937. Vidal's version of this controversy is found in "A Distasteful Encounter with William F. Buckley, Jr." on pp. 947–63 of this same volume.
8. Ibid., p. 942.
9. Vidal, "Encounter," p. 948.
10. Vidal, *Burr* (New York: Random House, 1973), p. 36.
11. Ibid., p. 430.
12. *National Review,* November 25, 1977, p. 1350.

Chapter Thirteen

1. *Inventing America* is the title of Garry Wills's provocative study of Jefferson's Declaration of Independence.
2. Macell D. Ezell, *Unequivocal Americanism* (Metuchen, N.J.: Scarecrow Press, 1977). This book is presented as a study of "Right-Wing Novels in the Cold War Era."
3. For Buckley's own discussion of Oakes's character, see "The American Look," in *A Hymnal,* pp. 409–12.
4. *Saving the Queen* (New York: Warner Books, 1977), p. 146; hereafter cited in the text as *S.*
5. Carey Winfrey, "Buckley at Home," *New York Times Book Review,* March 14, 1978, p. 36.
6. *Stained Glass* (New York: Warner Books, 1979), p. 38; hereafter cited in the text as *S.*
7. Saint Anselm's is "located on a line that once determined the geography of the West—the *limes,* at Cologne, between Rome and the Barbarians" (Ronald Berman, "The Virgin and the Dynamo," *National Review,* June 9, 1978, p. 726).

8. Ibid.

9. *Who's On First* (Garden City, N.Y., 1980), p. 9; hereafter cited in the text as *W*.

10. Jack Chatfield, "Exuberant Harmony," *National Review*, April 4, 1980, pp. 422–23.

11. See, for example, "The Moon and Bust?," in *The Jeweler's Eye*, pp. 67–70. Here, Buckley voices some reservations about America's mania to beat Russia to the moon.

12. At one point in *Who's On First*, John Foster Dulles says of a prospective Soviet satellite launch: "To travel in the public memory, in one year, from the country that gunned down Hungarian students to the country that launched a space program, with the obvious implications this has of a military nature, is an exercise in self-transformation" (p. 215).

13. *Marco Polo, If You Can* (Garden City, N.Y., 1982), p. 45; hereafter cited in the text as *MP*.

14. See Weeks's review of *Saving the Queen* in *The New Republic*, June 5, 1976, p. 28.

15. See Goodman's review of *Saving the Queen* in *New York Times Book Review*, January 11, 1976, p. 8.

Chapter Fourteen

1. I am focusing here on the conservative mainstream rather than on the followers of such fringe types as Ayn Rand, Murray Rothbard, Robert Welch, Lyndon LaRouche, and L. Brent Bozell.

2. At the risk of oversimplification, we may characterize these people as liberal on economics, moderate on social issues, and conservative on foreign policy.

3. Ross, *Literary Politicians*, p. 3.

4. Ibid., p. 5.

5. Among its other virtues, *The Unmaking of a Mayor* contains two of the more interesting paragraphs in the English language. The first (pp. 2–3) is an exposition on what Buckley calls the "marginal disutility of bloc satisfaction" (p. 2). In an elaborate cause-and-effect analysis, reminiscent of "for want of a nail the shoe was lost," the candidate recites a litany of New York City's ills beginning with double parking and progressing to the point where "you can't walk from one end of New York to another without standing a good chance of losing your wallet, your maidenhead, or your life" (p. 3). The second passage narrates the hypothetical plight of a "modern Justine" as she wrestles with the unpleasantness of life in New York (p. 32).

6. Jeffrey Hart, *The American Dissent: A Decade of Modern Conservatism* (Garden City, N.Y., 1966), p. 34.

Selected Bibliography

PRIMARY SOURCES

1. Books Written
Airborne: A Sentimental Journey. New York: Macmillan, 1976.
Atlantic High. Graden City, N.Y.: Doubleday, 1982.
Cruising Speed. New York Putnam, 1971.
Execution Eve. New York: Putnam, 1975.
Four Reforms. New York: Putnam, 1973.
God and Man at Yale. Chicago: Henry Regnery, 1951.
The Governor Listeth. New York: Putnam, 1970.
A Hymnal. New York: Putnam, 1978.
Inveighing We Will Go. New York: Putnam, 1972.
The Jeweler's Eye. New York: Putnam, 1968.
Marco Polo, If You Can. Garden City, N.Y.: Doubleday, 1982.
McCarthy and His Enemies (with L. Brent Bozell). Chicago: Regnery, 1954.
Rumbles Left and Right. New York: Putnam, 1963.
Saving the Queen. Garden City, N.Y.: Doubleday, 1976.
Stained Glass. Garden City, N.Y.: Doubleday, 1978.
United Nations Journal. New York: Putnam, 1974.
The Unmaking of a Mayor. New York: Viking, 1966.
Up From Liberalism. New York: Obolensky/McDowell, 1959.
Who's On First. Garden City, N.Y.: Doubleday, 1980.

2. Books Edited
The Committee and Its Critics. New York: Putnam, 1962.
Did You Ever See a Dream Walking: American Conservative Thought in the Twentieth Century. Indianapolis: Bobbs-Merrill, 1970.
Odyssey of a Friend: Whittaker Chambers' Letters to William F. Buckley, Jr. 1954–1961. New York: Putnam, 1969.
WFB [Sr.]—*An Appreciation* (with Priscilla L. Buckley). New York: Privately published, 1959.

3. Symposia Contributions
Campbell, Robert, ed. *Spectrum of Catholic Attitudes.* Milwaukee: Bruce Publishing Co., 1969.

Dialogues in Americanism. Chicago: Regnery, 1964.

Machlup, Fritz, ed. *Essays on Hayek.* New York: New York University Press, 1976, pp. 95–106.

4. Uncollected Essays (since 1978)

"Hollywood Piety." *National Review,* September 18, 1981, pp. 1091–93 (review of film *True Confessions*).

"Human Rights and Foreign Policy: A Proposal." *Foreign Affairs,* 58 (Spring 1980), 775–96.

"A Journal" (Part I). *The New Yorker,* January 31, 1983, pp. 55–56, 60–62, 64, 69–73, 76–84, 86–89.

"A Journal" (Part II). *The New Yorker,* February 7, 1983, pp. 46–48, 50–51, 53–54, 56–57, 59–60, 65–66, 68–72, 74–78, 80, 82, 84–87.

SECONDARY SOURCES

1. Biography and General Criticism

Dubois, L. Clayton. "The First Family of Conservatism." *New York Times Magazine,* August 9, 1970, pp. 10–11, 27–28, 30, 32, 34, 38. A generally favorable portrait of the Buckley family written during Jim's Senate campaign.

[Dubois, L. Clayton]. "Sniper," *Time,* November 3, 1967, pp. 70–72, 77–78, 80. A wide-ranging story on Buckley's career.

Hart, Jeffrey. *The American Dissent: A Decade of Modern Conservatism.* Garden City, N.Y.: Doubleday, 1966. An advocate's account of the conservative movement during *National Review*'s first decade.

King, Larry L. "God, Man, and William F. Buckley." *Harper's,* March 1967, pp. 53–61. A personality profile which concludes that Buckley is an amiable snob who lacks empathy for the common man.

Leo, John. "Very Dark Horse in New York." *New York Times Magazine,* September 5, 1965, pp. 8–9, 31–32, 34, 36. An amusing profile of Buckley as candidate for Mayor of New York City.

MacDonald, Dwight. "Scrambled Eggheads on the Right." *Commentary,* April 1956, pp. 367–73. An early denunciation of the editors of *National Review* as "half-educated provincials, . . . men from the underground, the intellectually underprivileged."

Markmann, Charles Lam. *The Buckleys: A Family Examined.* New York: William Morrow, 1973. An informative but superficial hatchet job on the entire family.

Merritt, Floyd Ernest. "William F. Buckley, Jr.: Spokesman for Contemporary American Conservatism—A Classical-Weaverian Rhetorical Analysis." Ph.D. dissertation, Ohio State University, 1973. Applies the rhetorical theories of Richard Weaver to an analysis of Buckley's speeches.

Nash, George H. *The Conservative Intellectual Movement in America Since 1945.*
    New York: Basic Books, 1976. A readable and scholarly history of post–
    World War II conservative thought.
Ross, Mitchell S. *The Literary Politicians.* Garden City, N.Y.: Doubleday,
    1978. A perceptive discussion of Buckley as one of several contemporary
    figures (Galbraith, Schlesinger et al.) "who have chosen to practice politics
    by writing books."
Vidal, Gore. "A Distasteful Encounter with William F. Buckley, Jr." In
    Smiling Through the Apocalypse, edited by Harold Hayes. New York: Dell,
    1969, pp. 947–63. Vidal's waspish account of his television debates with
    Buckley.
Wakefield, Dan. "William F. Buckley, Jr.: Portrait of a Complainer." *Esquire,*
    January 1961, pp. 49–52. An amusing character sketch written early in
    Buckley's career.
Willis, Garry. "Buckley, Buckley, Bow Wow Wow." *Esquire,* January 1968,
    pp. 72–76, 155, 158–59. A thoughtful and entertaining personality
    profile which focuses on one of Buckley's debates with Yale chaplain
    William Sloane Coffin.
————. *Confessions of a Conservative.* Garden City, N.Y.: Doubleday, 1979. A
    brilliant and engaging intellectual autobiography which includes a discus-
    sion of Wills's early years with *National Review.*
————. *Politics and Catholic Freedom.* Chicago: Regnery, 1964. A scholarly
    examination of the doctrinal force of papal encyclicals which uses the *Mater
    et Magistra* controversy as a point of departure.
Winfrey, Carey. "Buckley at Home." *New York Times Book Review,* May 14,
    1978, pp. 13, 36–37. An interview with Buckley which appeared shortly
    after the publication of *Stained Glass.*

2. On Specific Works

Berman, Ronald. Review of *Stained Glass. National Review,* June 9, 1978, pp.
    725–26. "Bill Buckley, like Henry Adams . . . , is writing about the
    Virgin and the Dynamo. The appalling literalness of the metaphor may be
    too much for coincidence."
Bundy, McGeorge. "The Attack on Yale." *Atlantic Monthly,* November 1951,
    pp. 50–52. A withering indictment of *God and Man at Yale;* finds Buckley
    to be "a twisted and ignorant young man whose personal views of econom-
    ics would have seemed reactionary to Mark Hanna."
Chatfield, Jack. Review of *Who's On First. National Review,* April 4, 1980, pp.
    422–23. Places Blackford Oakes in the tradition of the American hero: "A
    century ago he might have lit out for the territory before the rest, but in
    [our present age], . . . his movement is relentlessly eastward."
Eastman, Max. "Buckley Versus Yale." *American Mercury,* December 1951,
    pp. 22–26. A favorable review of *God and Man at Yale:* "Bill Buckley

throws a whole handful [of chalk] right at the teacher and right while he is looking."

Goodman, Walter. Review of *Saving the Queen*. *New York Times Book Review*, January 11, 1976, p. 8. "Our young agent's morale is excellent and his conscience unspotted; clearly this book was not written by a Catholic novelist."

Hentoff, Margot. Review of *The Governor Listeth*. *New York Review of Books*, December 3, 1970, pp. 19–20. "It appears that Mr. Buckley is beginning to take on the weight of middle-aged responsibility, sounding more often like a resilient prince of the Church than like a purifying spirit."

Moynihan, Daniel Patrick. Review of *Four Reforms*. *New York Times Book Review*, January 13, 1974, pp. 5–6. "The theme consistent in all his work is libertarian."

Reichley, James. Review of *Up From Liberalism*. *New Republic*, October 19, 1959, p. 27. "Mr. Buckley's proposition in this book appears to be that if he can prove that leading liberals are in the grip of some kind of 'mania,' he will thereby have demolished the liberal philosophy."

Sheppard, R. Z. Review of *Airborne*. *Time*, December 6, 1976, pp. 91–92. "Airborne . . . provides an excellent working definition of a conservative: someone who has something of spiritual or material value worth conserving."

Index

156